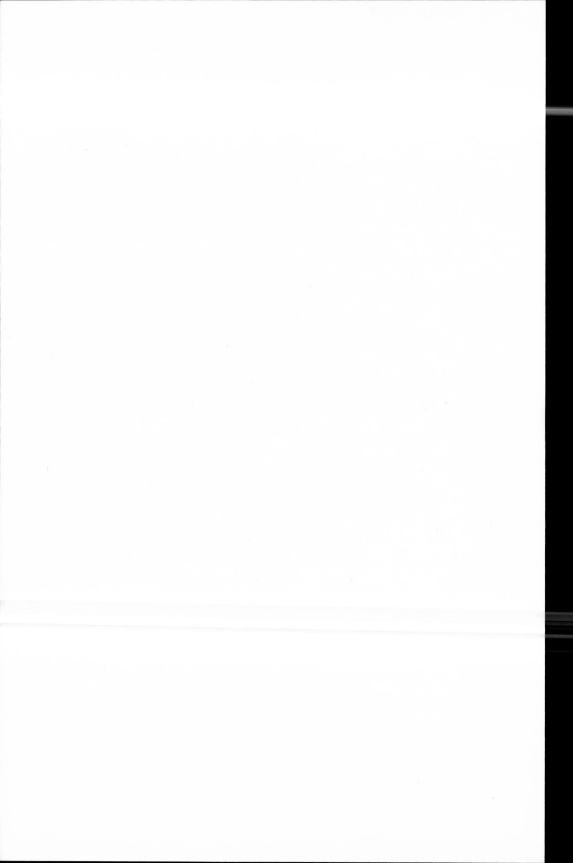

STRATEGIC FOCUS

A Gameplan for Developing Your Competitive Advantage

STRATEGIC FOCUS

A Gameplan for Developing Your Competitive Advantage

By Stephen C. Tweed

FELL PUBLISHERS, INC.
Hollywood, Florida

Library of Congress Cataloging In-Publication Data

Tweed, Stephen C.
    Strategic focus : a gameplan for developing your competitive
advantage / by Stephen C. Tweed.
        p.   cm.
    ISBN 0-8119-0651-5 : $17.95
    1. Strategic planning. 2. Competition. I. Title.
HD30.28.T84   1990
658.4'012--dc20

ISBN: 0-8119-0651-5

Manufactured in the United States of America
234567890

DEDICATION

This book is dedicated to my children, Jason, Jennifer and Jill,
for their continued love and support.

ACKNOWLEDGEMENTS

This book began as a personal goal early in my career, while still a technical writer at JOY Manufacturing company. It only moved from vision to reality at the urging of some very special people. A number of others made important contributions along the way.

A very deep and heartfelt thank you goes out to my good friends Nido Qubein and Tom Watson who urged me to begin this project, and helped me get started. To Pat Kunselman, Sue Hilton and Faith Findlay, on my staff at Tweed Corporation who typed and retyped the manuscript, and who helped me promote the book.

To Og Mandino, special thanks for helping me put together the proposal to publishers, and to Gerry Wallerstein, my literary agent who helped me select the right publisher.

To Allan Taber, Editor-in-Chief, and Donald Lessne, Publisher at Fell Publishers, Inc. for their guidance and support in producing the book.

To my good friends Larry Lottier and Mary Ellen Razanauskas who read early drafts of the manuscript, and gave me feedback.

To all of the executives who took time to answer my questions and give me examples, including Carl Heinz from JOY Technologies, Joseph B. Dahlkemper from the Joseph B. Dahlkemper Company, Inc., Chet Giermak from Eriez Magnetics, Wally Barnes, Bill Fenoglio and Stan Wells from the Barnes Group, John Knapp from Bowman Distribution, Dick Hines from Associated Spring, Len Carroll from First Seneca Bank - Integra Financial Systems, Dick Fisher and Donald Alstadt from Lord Corporation, Marty Eisert from Erie Insurance Group, Ruthanne Nerlich from the Visiting Nurses Association of Venago County, and Bob Sweet from Creative Pultrusions, Inc.

A special tanks to Mike Vance, and Jerry McNellis for teaching me storyboarding, the technique which has helped me create STRATEGIC FOCUS for myself and my clients.

My apology to all of the other people who have helped, and whose names have not been mentioned. You are not forgotten.

Very Best Regards,

Stephen C. Tweed
Oil City, Pennsylvania
March 28, 1990

CONTENTS

Chapter One

Chapter Two

Chapter Three

Chapter Four

Chapter Five

Chapter Six

Chapter Seven

Chapter Eight

Chapter Nine

Chapter Ten

Chapter Eleven

How to Keep Your Focus in Focus 159

Chapter Twelve

**Role of the Management Team in
Guiding Strategic Focus** 171

CHAPTER ONE

What Is Strategic Focus?

PURPOSE: *To define and clarify Strategic Focus as a necessary orientation for business and personal success in today's competitive marketplace.*

The biggest single problem facing most companies today is ... *LACK OF FOCUS!* Companies and their people are distracted and diluted by a variety of forces inside and outside the organization.

If companies are going to be successful competing in the global marketplace of the 1990's, they must concentrate their thoughts and efforts. They must focus.

Over the past fifteen years, I have worked with a variety of very successful entrepreneurial companies. I have studied many successful individuals, groups and organizations. The common denominator I have observed is the ability to focus. It is the ability to concentrate one's energy and thoughts on those few fundamentals required for success in a competitive situation.

Check it out yourself. Think of a highly successful person you know of in any field of endeaver: athletes, scientists, entertainers, business people. Every one of them has a high level of ability to focus on the fundamentals of his or her craft. They all have an

1

unusually clear mission or purpose, and they are able to direct their undivided attention at achieving their purpose. It is this singleness of purpose that makes them successful.

Leonardo DiVinci, Benjamin Franklin, Thomas Edison, Willie Mays, Vince Lombardi, Walt Disney, Ray Kroc, Thomas Watson Sr. They all had this rare ability to focus. Some of them were individual performers. Others ran large and complex organizations. But those large, complex successful organizations are made up of many smaller, highly focused business units. No matter how large or complicated the task, the ability to break that task down into small manageable pieces and to concentrate on one piece at a time is what makes the difference.

If you look up the noun *FOCUS* in the dictionary, you will find that it refers to a point at which rays of light, heat or other radiation meet after being refracted. This simple definition is often accompanied by a diagram of a lens.

A second definition is "a central point of attraction, attention or activity." The verb, *to focus*, means to bring to a focus or central point, to concentrate.

To be competitive in the world of business, a company must have not only focus, but Stragetic Focus. Strategic Focus is:

The process of concentrating thoughts and actions on those unique factors that will help your organization gain and sustain competitive advantage in the marketplace.

To understand Strategic Focus, we must first have a common understanding of strategy; and we must begin by bursting one old bubble. Strategy is not long range. Strategic planning and long-range planning are not synonymous. Strategy is synonymous with competitive advantage. Strategy is all about beating your competitor in the marketplace.

The American College Encyclopedic Dictionary defines strategy this way:

strat-e-gy, *n. pl.* -gies. 1. Also, stra-te-gics. Generalship; the science or art of combining and employing the means of war in planning and directing large military movements and operations. 2. The use, or a particular use, of this science or art. 3. Skillful management in getting the better of an adversary or attaining an end. The method of conducting operations, esp. by the aid of maneuvering or strategem.

strat-a-gem, *n.* 1. a plan, scheme or trick for deceiving the enemy. 2. any artifice, ruse or trick.

These definitions should clarify the point that strategy is not necessarily long range. If you can defeat the enemy on the battlefield tomorrow, the war is over. I'm sure you will agree, however, that in business, a strategy that can be sustained over a long period of time is probably better than a single victory in a market.

A classic example of shortterm Strategic Focus comes from Coach Joe Paterno and the Penn State University Nittany Lions. In 1986 Paterno had led his team to its second consecutive undefeated regular season. Standing between them and a National Championship were the University of Miami Hurricanes and their Heisman Trophy quarterback, Vinny Testaverde.

Miami was heavily favored to win as the two teams faced a showdown in the 1987 Fiesta Bowl in Tempe, Arizona. But Paterno and his defensive coordinator, Jerry Sandusky, had plans for Miami. They had studied film on the Hurricanes for exhausting hours. They decided they were going to focus on Miami's greatest strength, and turn it into a weakness.

Testaverde had thrown 116 consecutive passes in 1985 and 114 in 1986 without an interception. On January 2, 1987, Penn State intercepted five Testaverde passes, including one by Pete Giftopoulos at the goal line with nine seconds left, to clinch the victory and the National Championship.

The strategy Paterno and Sandusky developed was to jam the Miami receivers at the line, and to wallop them in the secondary as a penalty for catching the ball. As a result of that strategy Testaverde's receivers dropped seven passes. The Nittany Lions' defensive coverages were so well designed and disguised that Testaverde often seemed to be throwing blind.

Not only does Paterno excel at creating and implementing shortterm Strategic Focus; he's also terrific in the long term. As a result, he's the second winningest coach in the NCAA. One important area of Strategic Focus for Joe Paterno is the balance between athletics and academics. The one statistic he's most proud of is that over eighty percent of his players have graduated and received a college degree. That's an accomplishment that no other major football university can claim.

Long-range planning has for the last three decades been one of those popular phrases that has become almost a school of management. Long-range planning is what people tend to do when they don't know what else to do; yet it is a vital function. Organizations that don't plan find themselves working their way out of their markets and sleeping through technical revolutions.

Strategy is different from, but not antagonistic toward, long-range planning. Long-range planning, in fact, is one of the tools of strategic focusing. Companies that do not address planning for the future might find themselves out of focus ten years from now.

For example, audiologists who continue to follow the old plan of bringing in a patient, testing his or her ears and sending a prescription for hearing aids off to a laboratory in the next state, will find themselves with little business when on-site testing and construction of hearing devices is a reality. The popularity of one-hour eye tests and lens fittings should serve as a warning that today's competitive marketplace demands that health care keep up with technological advancements and busy schedules.

A lot of businesses get so caught up in day-to-day managing that they fail to plan for the future in a way that assures that their Strategic Focus will be viable five or ten years from now. Most of the businesses we have worked with were not engaged in a concentrated marketing war. Instead, they were fighting hundreds of brush fires, diluting their strength and thus their ability to compete. Throughout history, great battles were won by generals who were able to concentrate their forces and engage the enemy where he was weakest. They were able to focus their resources on a single point of battle. Hopefully, as a result of our consulting efforts, our clients are able to focus to concentrate their forces, and to sustain that concentration over the long haul.

Our working definition of strategy is designed with extended existence in mind. We define strategy as:

The actions that an organization must take in order to gain and sustain a significant competitive advantage in the marketplace.

In my consulting work with clients, I take this definition one step further. Strategic thinking is:

The process by which the top executives of an organization decide what actions to take in order to gain and sustain a significant competitive advantage in the marketplace.

There are several key words in this definition that I want to reinforce in your mind:

Process: Strategic thinking must be ongoing. It should not be a once-a-year exercise that people are forced to endure. Dr. Edward Freeman, Professor of Business Administration at the Colgate Darden Graduate School of Business, calls relying on long-term results an excuse. "Long term is a series of successful short-term achievements," Freeman contends.

Top executives: Strategic planning is done by top-level and line executives, not by a planning department. Since the top-level executives are entrusted with an organization's vision and goals, they also have the duty to interpret and make those visions and goals reality.

Action: Strategic thinking is focused on what needs to be done. It is action-oriented, not numbers-oriented. Jan Carlzon, President of Scandinavian Airlines System, says that strategic thinking is "a talent for rising above the details to see the lay of the land. The ability to understand and direct change..." [1]

Significant competitive advantage: Attention to important organizational issues determines the direction of the function we identify as strategic thinking. In order to maintain a significant competitive advantage, you must:

(1) Know who your customers are and what they expect.

(2) Know who your competitors are and what they have to offer.

(3) Differentiate your products or services from those of your competitors.

(4) Focus on the benefits of your products or services as perceived by your customers.

That brings us to probably the most important concept in the setting of strategy — and perhaps in all of business — **perception.**

Strategy is based on the perception of the customer. For your strategy to be effective, your customers must perceive that your product or service meets their needs more effectively than the products or services of your competitors.

This practical definition of strategy is based on my work with top organizational and corporate executives over the years. As I led Executive Strategy Retreats with management teams from major corporations, hospitals, medium-sized family-owned businesses, and professional associations, I saw the importance of the strategic thinking process. The more our discussions focused on strategy and competitive advantage, the easier it was to reach consensus. This meant it was easier to get the entire executive team moving in the same direction. And is is the top team moving simultaneously toward a significant competitive advantage that makes a company exceptional.

The problem sometimes is that business leaders are much more attuned to long-range planning than they are to strategic focusing. Therefore, when you say "Strategic Focus," their natural tendency is to think "long range planning."

There's a subtle, but important, distinction between the two. There's a long-range dimension to Strategic Focus. The objective of Strategic Focus is not simply to win a skirmish on a particular product or product line, or even in a set market on any given day, although that's part of it. The objective is to create the systems, approaches and methods that will consistently win battle after battle in the long war.

Let's look at how our definition of strategy and Strategic Focus fits with that of some of the top thinkers on the subject in the business field.

Kenichi Ohmae, a consultant with McKinsey and Company, and author of the book *The Mind of the Strategist*, says:

What business strategy is all about — what distinguishes it from other kinds of business planning — is, in a word, **competitive** advantage. Without competitors, there would be no need for strategy, for the sole purpose of strategic planning is to enable the company to gain, as efficiently as possible, a sustainable edge over its competitors. [2]

Dr. Alan J. Zakon, chairman of the board of the Boston Consulting Group, says:

Strategy begins with competitive advantage. Competitors control your profitability. Outstanding profitability, therefore, depends on sustainable competitive advantage. [3]

David A. Aaker, a strategic thinker from the University of California at Berkely and author of *Strategic Market Management*, included the following elements in defining business strategy:

- The product-market in which the business is to compete.
- The sustainable competitive advantage or advantages that will provide the business core.
- The distinctive competencies or assets which will be relied on to generate or maintain the sustainable competitive advantage. [4]

Tom Peters and Robert Waterman, Jr., co-authors of *In Search of Excellence*, contend in that book, "Great companies...are all driven by changing pressures in the marketplace." [5]

Peters and Waterman observe further that the chief difficulties in carrying through strategic functioning in the business arena are in the continuous adaptation and execution of a strategic plan.

More recently, in his book *Thriving on Chaos*, Peters is specific:

Tomorrow's successful corporation will be a collection of skills and capabilities ever ready to pounce on brief market anomalies. Any useful strategic...planning process must focus on the development and honing of these skills (which translates into readiness to seek and exploit opportunities), rather than emphasize static approaches to market development. [6]

The idea of strategy being focused on developing capabilities is reinforced by Ohmae when he says:

The job of the strategist is to achieve superior performance, relative to competition, in the key factors for success of the business....A successful strategy is one that ensures a better or stronger matching of corporate strengths to customer needs than is provided by competitors. In terms of these three key players (customers, competitors, company), strategy is defined as the way in which a corporation endeavors to differentiate itself positively from its competitors, using its relative corporate strengths to better satisfy customer needs. [7]

Craig Hickman and Michael Silva, authors of *Creating Excellence*, support this idea when they say, "Locating, attracting and holding customers is the purpose of strategic thinking. Without such a concrete goal, strategic thinking degenerates into an ivory tower experience." [8]

Competing for "Stakeholders"

With recent emphasis on the importance of an organization's strategy in a competitive marketplace, the question should be asked, "What are we competing for?" Too often we get so myopic as to think we are competing only for sales dollars, or for customers. In fact, every successful company is not only competing for sales and customers, but for stakeholders. Stakeholders are groups of individuals who have some stake in the success or failure of the enterprise. Every company has five traditional stakeholder groups: customers, employees, owners, suppliers, and community. The companies that will be most successful in the 1990's and beyond are those companies that do the best job of meeting the expectations of all their stakeholders.

That becomes a bit of a problem, and may even be a contradiction to the concept of Strategic Focus. But then, no one said this was going to be easy. Stakeholder groups often have mixed, or even conflicting, expectations. These conflicting expectations form the basis for the distraction and dilution that companies face.

NCR Corporation sponsored the First International Symposium On Stakeholders in 1988 to address this very issue. Although there are no easy answers, the participants agreed that there is clear evidence that companies which pay attention to the needs and expectations of all of their stakeholders are more successful than those companies which focus only on the needs of their owners, or customers.

We at Tweed Corporation have used the stakeholder concept in our strategic thinking process for several years and are glad to see the idea catching on across the business world.

The premise we follow in our consulting and strategic planning retreats is that organizations that consider and manage for all their stakeholders will be more successful than will those that manage only for their shareholders. As part of our Executive Strategy Retreat, we ask members of the strategy team to identify their stakeholders and outline the expectations of each stakeholder group. For most businesses, the stakeholders list includes customers, employees, shareholders, suppliers, the community, the government and other groups specific to particular companies.

I will go into how we conduct Executive Strategy Retreats in a later chapter, but first let's explore the stakeholder concept as it applies to strategic planning. Planning with stakeholders in focus ensures that management will allocate organizational resources to address the needs and expectations of the various stakeholder groups. It's a team attitude. The result of cooperation and stakeholder planning is to increase organizational value. Strategic stakeholder planning requires group members to work together to make a better company. It does not allow for various company segments to fight independently for a bigger block of the existing organization.

Effective Strategies Focus on Stakeholder Needs

When stakeholders' perceptions of their needs are at the center of an organization's planning and strategy, cooperation and trade-offs occur and a competitive edge is gained. Customers want quality and reasonable product prices. Employees want good working conditions, recognition, competitive salaries. Shareholders want efficient production and profits. Suppliers want to move their product at the best price. The community wants corporate involvement and financial support. All these stakeholder wants and needs must be considered in forming a strong organizational strategy.

Key to bringing a strategy together and making it work, however, is an organization's ability to focus on its competitive advantage.

Why Strategize If No Competition

Some strategic thinkers contend that if there is no competition, there is no need for strategy. Certainly competition demands that an organization sharpen its strategy and focus on its advantage in order to stay alive in today's marketplace. Companies that fail to think and plan strategically, even though they may have no current competition, leave the door unlatched for an intruder.

Many business leaders take a Pollyanna approach and say, "If we run a tight ship and do a good job with what it is that we do, we don't have to worry about competition," or "We don't have to worry about what our competitors are doing; we will just do a better job, and that will take care of them." Some will even say, "Our product is so unique, we don't have any competition." If the latter statement is ever true, it's a very short-term condition. If an organization has something that's selling and there's no competition, somebody is going to look around and say, "Hmmm, that's like having a license to steal. I want some of that, too."

The names Singer and Maytag were once synonymous to American homemakers with sewing and washing machines.

Young homeowners did not replace their ice boxes with refrigerators, they bought "Frigidaires."

Generations later Maytag's lonely repairman carried on the company's image of a producer of quality products with no match in the marketplace. Frigidaire has expanded to a large line of quality electrical products and continues to control a competitive market share. Companies like Brother, Necchi, Bernist, Pfaff , Viking, even Sears, have penetrated Singer's corner, however. The organization failed to focus on its competitive advantage in sewing machines. Singer today makes typewriters and computers and furniture, but none of those products lead their markets.

A company has lost its Strategic Focus when its management loses sight of their mission and the fundamental value provided by their products or services. When top executives in an organization fail to concentrate attention on their full list of stakeholders, they fail to think strategically.

KEY POINTS

(1) **Strategy is synonymous with competitive advantage.**

(2) **Strategic thinking:**
   - **Must be ongoing**
   - **Is done by top-level executives.**
   - **Is action-oriented.**

(3) **Perception is the most important concept in setting strategy.**

(4) **Managing for stakeholders is more productive than managing for shareholders.**

(5) **When top executives lose sight of the competition and customers, there is no strategy.**

NOTES:

[1] Jan Carlzon, *Moments Of Truth* Cambridge, Mass.: Ballinger Publishing Co., 1987), p. 35.

[9] Kenichi Ohmae, *The Mind of the Strategist* (New York, N.Y.: Penguin Books, 1982), p. 36.

[3] Alan J. Zakon, "The Two Sides of Strategy," *Perspectives*, 1986 (Boston: The Boston Consulting Group). p. 1.

[4] David A. Aaker, *Strategic Market Management* (New York, N.Y.: John Wiley & Sons). p. 4-5.

[5] Thomas J. Peters and Robert H. Waterman Jr., *In Search of Excellence* (New York: Harper & Row, Publishers, 1982). p. 100.

[6] Tom Peters, *Thriving on Chaos* (New York: Alfred A. Knopf, 1987). p. 510.

[7] Ohmae, *Mind*. pp. 91-92.

[8] Craig R. Hickman and Michael A. Silva, *Creating Excellence* (New York: New American Library, 1984). pp. 46-47.

CHAPTER TWO

How Focus Can Sharpen Your Competitive Edge

PURPOSE: *To demonstrate how organizations and individuals can be more successful by focusing their energies, resources and efforts. We will look at how focusing fits into the big picture — the overall operation — through specific examples from business, sports and science.*

Your value in the marketplace (and, hence, your success) will be directly proportional to how effectively you manage your resources and opportunities. To complicate matters, no business operates in a vacuum. So, if your competitors have more resources or manage their resources better, it dulls your competitive edge. In the increasingly competitive global marketplace, Strategic Focus is not an option — it's a necessity.

In my consulting work, I often hear the questions, "Why should we focus? Why can't our company be a broad, general purpose organization that meets the needs of many different customers with many different kinds of products and services?"

The answer is simple. You will be more successful if you focus. Focusing boosts effectiveness through concentration of efforts and resources where they will do the most good. Strategic focusing is the planning and executing of tactics that will always put you in your most advantageous position in relationship to all the forces that work against you in your attempts to achieve your goals. It is a truly unique individual or management organization that has the ability to focus, to concentrate on one issue or project until it is completed.

We are told that inventor/artist Leonardo DaVinci was not only brilliant in his ability to work in a number of different areas, but he had an amazing ability to concentrate on one project at a time. Benjamin Franklin, the printer, writer, politician, was also known for his ability to focus attention and efforts on one project at a time.

As I sit writing this chapter, The ABC-TV news program *Nightline* is on. Newsman Ted Koppel is interviewing American skaters Jill Watson and Peter Oppegard, winners of the bronze medal in pairs figure skating at the 1988 Winter Olympic Games in Calgary, Alberta, Canada. In response to Koppel's questions about preparation for their performance, both skaters talk about the importance of concentrating on the matter at hand.

"Jill and I both go into the rink about an hour before we perform," Oppegard said. "We look at the ice rink, look at the huge stadium that we are going to perform in, and then, gradually, within that hour, start to narrow and narrow our focus until, for myself, all I see is Jill and the ice. I don't see an audience. I don't see judges; just Jill and the ice and my reaction to Jill and her skating."

Watson echoed Oppegard's strategy. "The thing that you have to be able to do is concentrate, be able to focus down low enough that you can just take each element as it comes in the program and not get ahead of yourself."

The idea being used to improve performance in sports is to focus on the task at hand and not the result, according to Dr. Jerry May, sports psychologist for the U.S. ski team.

That idea transfers successfully into the business world. Tom Peters, author and co-author of several books on business and management including *In Search of Excellence, A Passion for Excellence* and *Thriving on Chaos*, has said that any executive has a thousand different things to do, but the most effective leaders are those who can concentrate on getting the two most important things on their list completed.

Dennis Connor, captain of the 1986-1987 America's Cup Team, makes sailing his business. The team that took the championship from Australia focused on excellence, according to Connor, who said he believed that attitude applied to any area of life. "Commitment to the commitment demands a very narrow focus," Connor pointed out. "You have to start with a meaningful goal, something of the utmost importance, and then put everything else aside until you achieve your goal. Wining breeds winning. The more you win the more used to it you become and the more hardened becomes your view of yourself. My theory is if you can visualize something, you can achieve it."

So, there you have it, Focusing 101 with Professor Connor. Applied either to the sports or the business world, the course description would read: Start out with a goal, assemble an organization, raise the money, tap the best technology the world has to offer, test, experiment with and try out seemingly crazy ideas — all with crystal clear focus.

Salespeople need the course, too. For them the course description reads: Establish a sales development program, find the perfect training site where you can blend all of the ingredients, seek out the best talent available and work, work, work.

Focus Prevents Waste

Establishing a focus allows an organization to set a course in a clear direction, to eliminate waste of efforts and resources. A company that knows its focus can avoid the floundering and false starts that occur in an organization whose people don't really know where they are going. In companies where every "good idea" is followed up, stakeholders don't have a clear picture of their organization's purpose; progress is slow and profits are down and efforts and resources are spent without measurable results.

One of my favorite stories on the importance of focusing is the story of Scandinavian Airlines and its president, Jan Carlzon.

Carlzon describes how he discovered the importance of focusing on a mission in a great detail in his book, *Moments of Truth.*[1]

Under Carlzon's leadership, SAS's mission was to be the world's best airline for business travelers. By focusing on a particular segment of the marketplace, Carlzon was able to guide the airline to superior on-time performance, superior scheduling, superior baggage-handling capabilities and all the other services necessary to meet the expectations of demanding business travelers.

Alvin Copeland, founder of Popeye's Famous Fried Chicken & Biscuits restaurants, focuses on serving dishes that will keep the establishment's more than 700 restaurants competitive with, or moving ahead of, other chicken houses. (At this writing, Popeye's, which is headquartered in New Orleans, is number three in the nation.)

Copeland delegated day-to-day operations to a group of division heads to save him time for creativity. He and staff chefs work uninterrupted several hours daily in Popeye's test kitchen, developing and testing recipes that will rival the offerings of such industry leaders as Col. Sanders. The company head and his cooks developed an acceptable crawfish dish in only two months, but took two years of concentrated effort to develop a biscuit recipe that met their high standards.[2] (The competition in the crawfish line may not be so intense as it is in the biscuit line.)

Focusing Makes Change Manageable

Every successful individual or organization develops a singular value in the marketplace. A close focus on that value creation translates into profitability, low overhead and ability to meet and manage change.

At the Dana Corporation, a Toledo, Ohio, manufacturer of components for the control and transmission of power, the focal point has been people — improving productivity through people.

During one recent year, Dana's Strategic Focus included these four internal aims:

(1) Improving quality continously to our customers

(2) Developing new definitions of manufacturing and distribution excellence

(3) Building a global business network of people and operations

(4) Growing the world-class skills of Dana people

By concentrating on these four goals and focusing on increasing productivity through people, Dana continues to develop as one of the best-run companies in America.

Another organization that has become tremendously successful through focusing is L.L. Bean, the catalog retailer of outdoor clothing and hunting shoes. The primary focus of the Bean company since it first introduced the Maine hunting shoe in 1923 has been external — absolute unqualified reliability. The guarantee on Bean products was, and still is, unconditional. A customer can send back a Bean product for any reason at any time and get a replacement or money back. You can actually wear something a year, decide that it is not holding up and send it back.

Obviously, to put that kind of a guarantee on products, many of which are not manufactured by L.L. bean, requires superior relationships with both suppliers and customers. Having that strong a focus on product reliability and providing the customer service to back it up has given the L.L. Bean company a significant competitive advantage in the marketplace.

The company has expanded from catalog sales to include a showroom that boasts some two million walk-in customers and is Maine's second-biggest tourist attraction. (The Atlantic Ocean ranks first, but Moosehead Lake and Mount Katahdin do not have as many visitors annually as the Bean store does.)

Focus Enables You to Communicate What You Have and What You Want

The power of Strategic Focusing is evident in the location of the International Furniture Market in the town of High Point, North Carolina.

Twice a year, between 20,000 and 30,000 furniture buyers from all over the world descend for ten days on that town of

70,000 population. For years, the town had hosted a regional furniture market but would not have emerged as the international organization and dominant market force that it is had it not been for the people in the community. There are not enough hotel and motel rooms within 100 miles of the central North Carolina town to accommodate such a crowd of business people. Probably one-third of the buyers stay in private homes in the area. That's support from the local community. The people are important stakeholders in the institution. If the area residents had risen up in indignation at the inconvenience caused by crowded roads and restaurants and had refused to give up their guest rooms to temporary boarders, the market could not function at its present level.

When you talk about increasing your competitive edge, you are talking about taking full advantage of all the resources you have available and using those resources in a way that your customers find more desirable than anything they can get from your competitors.

Taking advantage of your resources has to do with quality. It has to do with productivity. It has to do with financial investment and capitalization. It has to do with employee relationships, with community relationships, with supplier and vendor relationships. It has to do with everything that in any way impacts on your business.

The market element is the key element, but it's not the total picture. When you talk about Strategic focus, you are talking about running a total organization.

The leaders in developing the International Furniture Market knew precisely what they were trying to do. Because they were so focused, they were able to communicate that purpose to the people in the community and to muster their support. They were able to talk about what it would men to individuals and businesses within the community to have a multi-million dollar event located in the small city.

One way the market organizers captured the lucrative show for the small, little-known city was to focus externally on what the various fragmented elements, the regional furniture markets, meant to such communities around the country as Chicago,

Dallas and Atlanta. They said, "Look how much money is being spent in those cities and just think what it would be like if we could have all that money spent here. It's a drop in the bucket to a big city, but it would really have significant meaning to our community to have that kind of money coming in. Consider how many job opportunities it will provide for this community."

Within the furniture-making industry, organizers communicated what they had to offer by saying, "Look how this will centralize your marketing efforts and, therefore, save enormous amounts of money and energy and give you a competitive edge. Many manufacturers hated the market organizers' tactics but could not ignore the advantages of supporting the idea.

Even big names in the furniture world like Broyhill and Thomasville closed their expensive local show rooms and spent millions of dollars moving their selling production to High Point, because that was where the action was, and if they were to be competitive, they had to be where the buyers were.

The one theme that market strategists kept hitting over and over and over was "This is the International Furniture Trade Show. You may show your furniture at High Point and Chicago or High Point and four or five regional markets, but you cannot survive in the furniture business if you ignore the international market, which happens to be located in High Point."

The existence of an international market came about because someone had the insight to recognize an opportunity. Furniture salespeople cannot take samples on the road and show buyers how the items would look in their rooms, so they built all the big rooms in one location, and twice a year they decorate them with the newest products in the line.

Periodically, one or another of the regional market cities, hungry for more action and with big resources to back them, pledges to take the market away from High Point, bout so far the committed little community continues to outstrategize the big boys.

External Focus Assures Loyalty

H & R Block, the tax preparation people, are an example of

what can happen when a company fixes its focus. Henry and Richard Bloch not only invented the tax preparation industry, they still basically own it more than thirty years later. Originally, the Bloch brothers operated a certified public accounting business that handled tax returns as part of a wide range of accounting services. According to Henry, his brother wanted to discontinue the tax return service because it required them to work long hours during the early months of each year and interfered with the needs of their regular accounting clients.

At a client's suggestion, however, the Blochs decided to focus their energy and expertise on tax preparation instead of abandoning the service. They had anticipated that the tax business would help their basic accounting service through word-of-mouth advertising and by generating referrals. It had the opposite effect. They sold the accounting business to a group of employees and centered their attention on developing an individual tax preparation business. The rest of the story is history. One in ten American tax payers look to H & R Block to prepare their annual return forms. Henry Bloch says the company's only significant competitor is the individual who insists on completing his or her own tax return.

How have they built such an empire?

"We'll look for most any excuse to do almost anybody's tax return free the first year because we know we're going to get eighty percent of them back after that," Henry said. (They do such things as giving free tax returns to high school seniors as Christmas presents.) "Preparing your taxes is strictly a habit. What you do one year you just keep doing."[3]

Examples of companies that have gained success through Strategic Focus are not limited to huge, well-known organizations. Early in my career, I had the opportunity to work with Joy Manufacturing Company, now known as Joy Technologies, Inc.

Joy has been able to dominate the domestic underground coal mining machinery industry by concentrating on the design and manufacture of equipment for the face extraction and haulage of coal from underground mines. Their focus on a specific market segment and on high product reliability has given Joy a dominant market share in all of the product lines that it manufactures and sells from its Franklin, Pennsylvania, facility. That dominance extends to the industry in South Africa and Australia. Joy is also making significant market progress in Great Britain and Europe.

What we keep seeing in each of these examples is that organizations grow and prosper when they identify and focus their attention on satisfying the needs of their stakeholders. That's when they develop a competitive advantage in the marketplace.

USAir Group, which originated as a small regional air carrier headquartered in Pittsburgh, Pennsylvania, pioneered the use of commuter airlines to feed its Pittsburgh hub. As governmental deregulation hit the airline industry in the early 1980s, many larger fliers changed their route structures, concentrating on long hauls and eliminating short hops. USAir took the opposite approach, continuing its service to small communities. As a result of their focus, USAir could serve some small markets with no competition and other markets with minimal competition. They also established the Allegheny Commuter System to feed major connecting hubs in the area. New Englanders can board a USAir commuter in their local community, fly into a larger facility, and make connections by USAir jet to almost any other major city in the country.

By focusing on a particular niche and providing reliable service, USAir managed to dominate the Northeastern market and to remain profitable during a period when many larger lines were losing millions of dollars. Piedmont Aviation, based in Winston-Salem, North Carolina, followed the same strategy successfully in the Southeast sector of the United States, as did Pacific Southwest Airlines on the West Coast. The two companies recently merged with USAir Group to solidify a strong market share against such industry giants as American, Delta, TWA, United and Pan Am.

Even Individuals Can Focus Effectively

Christopher Whittle's story is indicative of what can happen when a project is launched with a clear focus.

Whittle and a college friend, Phillip Moffitt, started a campus magazine at the University of Tennessee during the '60s. They aimed their publication at readers between thirteen and thirty years of age. The magazine prospered and the young men expanded their attention to include other publications, but each project was aimed at a clearly defined audience.

Whittle now heads his own company, but his enterprises still exhibit the attention to focus that the earlier publishing efforts had. *Road Trips*, a glossy piece with pictures and short travel articles about places accessible by vehicle, is a specialty publication for Chevrolet customers. It has one advertiser Chevrolet; a targeted audience car owners; and a captive audience persons who are waiting for vehicle repairs.

The entrepreneur, located in Knoxville, Tennessee, has produced other focused publications aimed at persons waiting in doctors' offices, pet owners who frequent veterinarians; offices, college students and high school students.

Most of Whittle's magazines are free and not widely known. *Top Line* is directed to small-business owners. *Southern Style* is for Southern women. At this writing, he was planning to launch *Special Reports*, six magazines issued quarterly for doctors; waiting rooms. Each publication would be focused on a narrow subject both in its printed material and ads. The subjects were to include: families, health, sports, living, personalities and fiction. One of the keys to Whittle's Strategic Focus was the idea that doctors who subscribed to *Special Reports* could have no more than two magazines by other publishers in their racks.[4]

Another person who has become highly successful in his business as a result of Strategic Focus is Nido Qubein. Qubein came to the United States from Lebanon at the age of seventeen. He had fifty dollars in his pocket and could not speak English. By concentrating his energies on becoming an effective speaker and communicator, he has built a multi-million dollar public speaking and consulting business headquartered in High Point, North Carolina. Tom Watson, senior editor and vice president of the editorial division at Creative Services, calls Qubein the most focused person he has ever met.

What Happens When Organizations Fail to Focus?

We can go on citing positive examples of organizations whose corporate value has been enhanced through their ability to focus, but let's also consider what has happened to some well-known companies that lost sight of their mission.

The most obvious examples of self destruction through failure to focus were the conglomerates of the '60s and '70s. In their striving for high growth and profitability, the conglomerates were tempted to acquire any business which appeared to meet their return-on-investment criteria. For a short while, many of these companies maintained a fast growth mode and appeared to be successful. However, their inability to manage their diversity soon became evident. By the late '70s and early '80s, many of the high-growth companies had to sell off acquisitions and trim down to the basic business in which they had started.

Beatrice Foods is a good example of the sudden-growth-sudden-cutback syndrome. Beatrice acquired a large number of companies outside their traditional food-oriented line. In 1986, Beatrice was taken private in a $6.2 billion leveraged buy-out. Within two years of the purchase, the corporation's new owners had sold ten subsidiaries that did not fit their vision of the future for Beatrice.

Another food-oriented company that got away from its focus was Gerber, the leading manufacturer and distributor of baby food. Gerber sought to diversify into other products and businesses — some totally unrelated to children. The company's management quickly recognized problems from its lack of focus and pulled back to basic baby food production.

We talked earlier about several airlines whose concentration on a narrow niche resulted in big growth and high market pay off. Braniff Airlines had an opposite experience.

In his book *Splash of Colors*,[5] writer-pilot John J. Nance described the downfall of Braniff International. Braniff, Nance said, overextended itself and lost sight of its basic customer service strategy through eagerness to expand into long-haul routes. The line lost customers and was ultimately forced into bankruptcy.

Exxon Corporation was this country's largest oil company at one time. That success would not carry over into their attempts to branch out of the oil field, however. Exxon created a subsidiary, a venture capital group, to innovate and develop new products. Exxon Office Systems, a spinout of the subsidiary group, got off to a good start with small computers and office typewriters, but were never able to compete effectively with IBM and other major office product companies.

Long-time retail giant W. T. Grant was forced into bankruptcy and eventual liquidation when it lost sight of its customers in terms of product quality and service.

Strategic Focus Creates Value

Adam Smith did not call it strategic planning more than 200 years ago. But that is what the Scottish economist described when he said that the function of business is to identify a need for a product or service, determine a fair price to charge for it and then figure out how to make it for less. Smith had identified the creation of value.

Companies that focus on creating value for a specific target market are able to survive and grow. The more focused a company is on creating value, the more successful it becomes.

Evidence substantiates the theory that focus pays off in profitability. According to a study conducted between 1977 and 1981 of 170 U. S. companies, about forty percent of the companies had a clear value-creating focus. Those companies averaged a 16.9% return on equity over the five-year period. In contrast, the companies without a clear focus earned only 12.8% on equity.

Tight focus is a powerful source of profitability. By articulating the core of a company — its corporate values, its value-creating focus — and testing that focus against reality, an organization can discover its potential to gain and sustain a competitive advantage in the marketplace.

In other words, when your organization defines its corporate values, principles and philosophies — when you know what you are doing and why you are successful — you can determine what requires change. It's when you don't know why you are successful that random change sneaks into a company, performance falls off and no one knows quite what is wrong.

Focus allows us to manage change. Without focus, the cart can get ahead of the horse; your corporation can find itself being managed by change. Focus keeps managers managing businesses, not administering them.

To be effective, in short, you must create value. You must create a statement of purpose that defines your real value-creating focus. And if you want to grow and diversify, growth and diversity must be within that focus. To accomplish successful growth, you must keep testing reality to insure that your value creation matches what the marketplace needs.

KEY POINTS

(1) **Strategic focusing boosts effectiveness through concentration of efforts and resources where they will do the most good.**

(2) **Focus makes change manageable.**

(3) **Focus enables you to communicate more precisely what you have to offer and what you want from others.**

(4) **Organizations survive and grow when they focus on creating value for a specific target market.**

(5) **Growth without focus may result in failure.**

NOTES:

[1] Jan Carlzon, *Moments of Truth* (Cambridge, Mass.: Ballinger Publishing Co., 1987).

[2] *USA Today*, April 11, 1988, sec. B, p. 4.

[3] "Taxman Henry Bloch," *INC.*, Dec., 1987. pp. 35-42.

[4] *USA Today*, March 10, 1988, sec. B, p. 7.

[5] John J. Nance, *A Splash of Color* (New York: W. M. Morrow, 1984).

CHAPTER THREE

Strategic Focus Begins with Vision

PURPOSE: *To demonstrate how to create Strategic Focus by creating a strategic vision for the future.*

Strategic Focus begins with vision. To develop and maintain Strategic Focus, you must zero in on who you are, what your business is and where you are going. You have to understand your real purpose for existence.

Winston Churchill once said, "One must always look ahead, but it is difficult to look farther than one can see."

That is especially true in today's business climate. Our world is changing so rapidly that it is often difficult to see into the future. Where some companies once predicted their future five years in advance, today many companies can't predict what will happen in the next ninety days.

Probably the single biggest cause for the lack of Strategic Focus in large publicly held companies today is the rash of mergers, acquisitions, and leveraged buyouts. Nothing takes a person's eye off the focus of serving the customer any quicker than the threat of an unfriendly takeover.

The reason manufacturing companies are having trouble making quality products is that top executives don't want to focus on the fundamentals of making things and selling things. They want to do deals. It's more exciting. The reason hospitals don't focus on patient care and quality service is that top administrators and physicians are busy doing deals and joint ventures.

The only way for an organization to gain and sustain competitive advantage over the long term is to focus on the fundamentals of the business, and meet the needs of customers. The way to create that Strategic Focus is to create a clear vision for the future of the business and to communicate that vision to all employees.

In our work with top executive teams in developing competitive strategies, we have identified five types of vision that a company should define:

(1) The Business Vision
(2) The Values Vision
(3) The Performance Vision
(4) The Competitive Vision
(5) The Focus Vision

Each of these five types of strategic vision leads us to a key element of the overall business strategy that will lead to competitive advantage.

The Business Vision

The first fundamental decision any business organization must make is to answer the question, "What business are we in?" I am constantly amazed at how many companies have not clearly defined their core business.

There are two parts to the business vision. First is the Mission, and second is the Purpose. The mission of a company defines *what* business that company is in, and perhaps more importantly what business it is *not* in. Purpose defines *why* a company exists. These two statements are very closely related. Some companies write separate statements of mission and purpose. Others include both ideas in the same statement.

When I describe the mission of a business to a client group, I draw a box on a piece of flip chart paper. Inside the box I write the word mission.

MISSION
The business we are in
The business we are NOT in

A well-written mission statement is like this box. It clearly defines what our business is, and what it is not. Only when we know what our business is NOT, can we focus on what our business is.

When Jan Carlzon took over the helm of Scandanavian Airlines in 1980, the company was in serious difficulty and losing millions of dollars. One of Carlzon's first efforts was to rewrite the mission of the company. He said, the company's mission was "to be the best airline in the world for the frequent business traveler." He made it clear that their business was not tourists, package handling or charter services. The focus was the frequent business traveler.

When Bob Townsend took over Avis Rent-a-Car, he rewrote the mission, "to be the fastestgrowing, most profitable company in the business of renting and leasing motor vehicles without drivers." Avis is not a bus company. It is not a limousine company. It is not a transportation company. It is a rent-a-car company.

When Ren McPherson took over at the Dana Corporation, the company developed the mission "to be the leading designer, manufacturer,and marketer of components for the control and transmission of power, worldwide." Dana makes components, Not completely assembled power equipment. Dana makes parts for the control and transmission of power, not for the power source or the power application. Dana makes universal joints, drive shafts and transmissions. They make parts for diesel engines, but not the engines. They make parts for trucks, but they don't make trucks.

In each of these three cases, there are logical business extensions which these companies could get into. The focused company clearly understands what business it is in and what businesses it is not in. The hard part is where to draw the line and how to avoid stepping over the line.

How to Write a Mission Statement

When I facilitate Executive Strategy Retreats, one of the first things we do is rewrite the company's mission statement. Some companies don't have one. Others have a general statement that doesn't really define the business.

We begin by storyboarding the key concepts of the business. Storyboarding is a technique we use for making ideas visible. It will be described in more detail in Chapter Six.

I begin by putting the following questions up on the storyboard:

- What do we want to be (as an organization)?
- What is our primary product or service?
- Who will use our product or service?

Using techniques of creative thinking, the group of executives then puts up lists of cards answering each of these questions. We talk about what our business is. Then I put up a header card that reads, "Non-Business." We make a list of businesses we could be in, but are not. Then we continue the discussion, talking in specific terms about what our business is, and is not.

Next, I have each person in the room write a draft mission statement. Each person reads his or her statement to the group. Then we collect the drafts and give them to a missionwriting team of three or four people. The mission writing team goes into another room and writes a discussion draft of the mission, using the best ideas from all of the participants.

When the writing team comes back with a discussion draft, the whole group reviews the draft, tears it apart and puts it back together. This is the working draft, which is still subject to review and discussion at a later meeting.

I have found that once a top-executive team goes through this exercise of defining its business, the rest of the strategy-setting process goes much more smoothly, and it is easier to reach

concensus about how the company will compete in the marketplace.

The Power of Purpose

The second part of the business vision — Purpose — describes why the company does what it does. Often, the statement
of purpose defines the company's contribution to society.

My thinking on the importance of purpose began in the
summer of 1987 with a speech by David McNally at the National
Speaker's Association Conference. McNally outlined a life of
financial ups and downs in which he made and lost fortunes
because his life had no purpose.

After graduating from high school at age seventeen, McNally,
an Australian, entered the work force. By nineteen he had
formed his own company, and by twenty-six was the multi-mil-
lionaire owner of a successful business, with all the amenities that
go with wealth. He traveled internationally. He owned a huge
home with a tennis court and a swimming pool and drove a Rolls
Royce.

By age twenty-eight, McNally was flat broke and deeply in
debt. "I don't remember setting that goal, but I achieved it
marvelously," he reported.

McNally crawled out of bankruptcy and created another
successful business, but he found that money itself had no
meaning, and he left that business as well. It was not until he
realized the power of having a purpose, McNally says, that he
began to gain satisfaction from his achievements.

One of the Australian's comparisons which has stuck with me
was the difference between purpose and goals. Purpose answers
the question of why we are who and where we are, while goals
are what we seek for ourselves. "Those people who lose sight of
purpose, and focus only on their goals, tend not to be successful,"
he said. "Oh, they may achieve the goal, but they really don't
achieve satisfaction in life."

It's the same in business. An organization needs both a
purpose and goals. Goals are the supporting elements of your

purpose. An organization that gets a true heading and sets its sights on its purpose will accomplish its goals along the way.

McNally illustrated that point by holding up one hand and designating it as purpose. We could focus clearly on that hand. But when he held up the other and called it goals and asked us to focus on both, we found our eyes shifting from one to the other. CEO's I interviewed while researching this book agreed that when a company focused on its purpose, the goals took care of themselves.

Your Purpose Is Not Just to Make a Profit

I suppose we've all heard business people say that the purpose of their organization is to make a profit for their shareholders. The results of my interviews contradicted that view. The point which I heard most frequently in successful companies was that their purpose was to serve the customer. By serving the customer satisfactorily, these companies served all the other stakeholders as well.

Stan Wells, Chief Financial Officer for The Barnes Group, Inc., a Bristol, Connecticut, based FORTUNE 500 manufacturing and distribution company, makes an interesting observation about this. It is particularly interesting coming from a finance guy. Stan says, "Financial results are not a goal themselves. They are the result of doing operational things like quality and service right. If we do those things extremely well, and if we are patient enough, the financial results will follow just like night follows day."

Before workers, customers, suppliers or the community will become stakeholders in an organization, they have to understand and buy into the company's purpose. And before they commit, they have to answer the following questions to their own satisfaction:

(1) What is our business?

(2) Why are we here?

(3) What is our long-term benefit to society?

(4) How does what we do make a difference in the world?

The answers to those questions will clarify the organization's purpose. People want to do meaningful work. They want to make a difference with their lives. Working for an organization with a clear purpose brings meaning to work and ultimately to life itself.

It's the responsibility of a company's top-level management to communicate purpose so that potential stakeholders will want to buy in and so that they do not have a short-sighted vision of the ultimate target.

People can get so concerned with their own goals that they lose sight of the reason behind those goals. They fail to focus on the purpose. When this happens, workers just want their paycheck; suppliers want to move raw materials; vendors want to handle your finished product at a profit; shareholders want a dividend check; and the community wants a contribution. And when everybody loses sight of the purpose, they become mere makers of profit rather than a source of service to customers and to the community.

Managers with insight and foresight continually talk the mission and the overriding purpose of their organization. They manage and direct the performance process and build company spirit through encouraging relationships within departments and between workers and management. They promote creativity, sharing, and collaboration and give their people space to grow and contribute. Such an attitude gets everybody involved and heading toward the same destination — the big purpose.

In drawing up a company purpose, Joy Technologies recognized the historical contribution of tool makers to society. The company arrived at its purpose this way:

> Carl Heinz, president of the Worldwide Mining Machinery Group of Joy, discovered an article on the importance of the tool-maker's role in world history. The piece described how, in order to survive, most ancient people were farmers.

> Then someone invented the plowshare. The tool made the inventor's life easier and he began to make plowshares for other farmers.

> The agrarian society became more productive, allowing

some members to move into occupations other than growing food. Some people created art works, some wrote music. Some individuals decided to care for the health of others, while some taught the newly developed skills to young people.

"Being a tool maker is something that all of our people could identify with," Heinz said. "So we created the purpose of being the tool makers for the mining industry."

There's another factor in the story of how the company arrived at its purpose:

Company founder Joe Joy was, in fact, a coal miner. Joy hated the backbreaking, dangerous work of digging coal and loading it by hand, so he invented a mechanical loading machine to dip loose chunks of the natural fuel from the mine floor into wagons for transportation outside the tunnels.

"Today the purpose of Joy Mining Machinery is to create tools for the underground coal miner to make it safer for the miner and more productive for the company. The result is reducing the cost of energy for the people of the world," Heinz said.

Managers with an understanding of the importance of organizational purpose will continually communicate the mission on a personal level for subordinates. A cohesiveness develops when employees stop seeing their jobs narrowly — as screw putter inners or oilers or clerk typists or bookkeepers or salespeople — and start seeing their roles as contributing to the overall purpose of the company.

Joy Technologies reinforces its purpose among employees by providing opportunities for people in all levels of the organization to visit miners in their underground workplace. The company president stated that when engineers and factory workers alike see how their machines are used and how they increase the safety and productivity of the coal miner, they develop a much deeper appreciation for the importance of their purpose.

In his book, *The Marketing Imagination*, Ted Levitt says the purpose of business is to create and keep customers.

> Who with a palpable heartbeat and minimal sensibilities will go to the mat for the right of somebody to earn a profit for its own sake. If no greater purpose can be discerned or justified, business cannot morally justify its existence.[1]

An organization's statement of purpose should contain the basic convictions on which management bases its decisions and actions. Successful businesses are winners because their management knows where the company is going. Management has a knowledge of the various stakeholder wants on which to develop a strategy and a stated purpose to shoot for.

Levitt says that a strong statement of purpose provides guidance and moral merit for management, and predicts failure for companies whose policies are tied to their own convenience rather than to the convenience of customers. "To say that a company should attract and hold customers forces facing the necessity of figuring out what people really want and value, and then catering to those wants and values."[2]

David McNally supports that theory when he says that "customers do not exist to help you achieve your goals and to make a profit, but if you help them meet their needs, you can achieve whatever you wish."

Chet Giermak, president of Eriez Magnetics, the world leader in magnetics and vibratory applications, says that his company always puts people before profits, and "we get awfully good people and very good profits."

Eriez has been in business for more than fifty years and has made a profit every year except 1983. "We could have made money in '83 if I would have laid people off, but I wouldn't do it because I believed that we needed the people for the future, and it was important for them to believe me and trust me," Giermak said.

The company publishes a statement as a guide for strategic planning and focus and for conducting business. The Eriez "Fundamental Principle" says the company's aim is:

Using the Golden Rule as a guide — to build a worldwide

organization that will give OUR CUSTOMERS high quality products and services at a favorable price commensurate with good service before and after sale; OUR ASSOCIATES the best possible job opportunity, work satisfaction, happiness and security; and OUR STOCKHOLDERS a reasonable continuing return on their investment. Recognizing our social responsibility to THE COMMUNITIES in which we operate, we will strive to conduct our affairs in such an efficient, capable and friendly manner that everyone with whom we come in contact will be happy to be associated with us.

The Eriez business mission is more specific:

To conduct a growing and profitable worldwide enterprise specializing in advanced technological aspects of magnetic and vibratory separation, product purification, pollution abatement, screening, metal detection, reclamation, controlled material movement and minerals beneficiation.

To utilize the technical capabilities of the Company and enhance the profit producing potential through seeking Research and Development contracts that will lead to equipment sales.

For the foreseeable future, plan to operate Eriez as a privately-held Company in which Eriez management and directors will retain operational and equity control.

In his company's purpose, Joseph B. Dahlkemper, founder of a chain of catalog showrooms, expresses a concern for making a contribution to his community. On the way to fulfilling that purpose, all the Dahlkemper stakeholders are being satisfied.

Dahlkemper reports that he started the business with one purpose survival. He was twenty-eight years old and had three children and a fourth on the way when the company he worked for closed. In a venture requiring courage and determination, he started his own retail sales business.

He began by purchasing giftware items from a wholesaler some sixty miles away. With no money to afford inventory,

Dahlkemper displayed all his merchandise in a small store front, and sold over the counter. At the close of business each day, he listed the items he had sold, emptied his cash drawer, and drove the 120-mile round trip to replenish his stock for the next day's business.

Dahlkemper survived the ordeal and his company grew. Within three years he showed a profit. So he set a new goal. His consuming purpose was to make enough money to send his children to the colleges of their choice.

"I never achieved that goal," he said. "By the time I could afford to send my children to the college of their choice, I had acquired the wisdom that, if they paid their own way, they would appreciate it more." (The Dahlkemper kids did pay their own college expenses and they do appreciate their father's attitude. They all still work in the family business.)

So, once again, the Erie, Pennsylvania, businessman changed his purpose — this time looking beyond survival and family needs. He saw local Gannon University as providing an opportunity for his company to impact its community. He made a $2 million contribution to the campus to expand the school of business there.

"John F. Kennedy made his contribution to the country. I have to settle for making a contribution to my community," Dahlkemper said. "If life is good to you, you have to put something back. I could have taken that $2 million and willed it to my children, but they already have good jobs and a company that they will own to insure them financial security."

By setting an idealistic purpose, the Joseph B. Dahlkemper Company has been able to satisfy all its stakeholders. They furnish employment in nine retail locations, buy from a wide range of suppliers, sell quality products at competitive prices, insure profits to shareholders, contribute to community growth and improvement and assure that quality educational opportunities are available for their children and the children of their stakeholders.

Lane Nemeth also answered a high calling when she established her toy business. When Nemeth discovered that top quality educational toys such as those used in early education programs were not available to the average family, she set out to rectify the situation. Her mission: "To distribute toys that develop a child's curiosity, creativity and intellect."

Since 1977, the former educator has handled a line of toys through a direct distribution plan comparable to Tupperware's and Mary Kay's technique. With a sales force composed primarily of young housewives, she stages in-home display/demonstration "parties." Nemeth's original goal was to improve the way children are reared, but she soon expanded it to include improving the lives of women as well. Some of her independent salespeople earn more than $200,000 annually.

On the way to achieving her purpose, Nemeth has fulfilled the needs of all her stakeholders.

Here's How You Draw Up a Purpose

A good purpose voices the basic attitudes, assumptions and convictions about why your organization exists. It is a statement on which management bases its decisions and actions.

Remember also that the basic purpose forms a framework for an organization's design and focus. A good way to start toward formulating a purpose, therefore, is for each person on the executive team to make a list of what, in his view, is important for the organization. Write down:

(1) Why does our organization exist?
(2) What do we want to accomplish?
(3) What is our company's overall contribution to society?
(4) What is it about our company that makes our work meaningful?

The responses will range everywhere from the idealistic, "I want this company to make an impact on peace in the world," to the light, "Lord, let me make enough money to retire while I can still play eighteen holes of golf every day."

Write them all down. You can use them when you start to structure your formal statement. Of course company executives want to retire rich at a young age. Who doesn't? Profits are stated or implied in most organizational statements of purpose. They may read something like, "Through the development and sale of the highest quality product available on today's market, we expect to create profits adequate to promote and maintain the growth and health of Widgetry International, support community development, etc., etc., etc."

Statements of purpose aren't meant to be specific, but idealistic. They reflect what is important to an organization, guide strategic decision making, provide for creativity, project an image, speak a philosophy by which everyone connected with a company can live. Mission and strategy provide the specifics to keep everyone going the same direction at the same pace.

As you begin to pull together the goals and aspirations listed by the group a good mission statement, a reason for existing, a purpose, will become evident. And once the statement is drawn up, it will serve as the foundation for all activity within the organization.

Evidence of positive results from focusing on purpose rather than on profits come from the Marriott organization, and no one will quibble with its success. The Marriotts' biographer says of Willard (Bill) and Allie Marriott and their management of their Hot Shoppes that they:

> ...didn't care about running a restaurant, per se....They were in the restaurant business — to turn out a product of quality, to serve the public, to keep prices low and still show a profit, to grow naturally and logically from the inside out.[3]

Although when something was needed, the Marriotts sought the right person or group to do the job, they reportedly never lost sight of the value of the personal touch in running a business. Biographer O'Brien reports that in the early days of the Marriott organization the owner visited each store daily, talked with employees, inspected facilities and introduced himself to customers, asking them what they liked and did not like about the business. He continually told his people: "Work hard, keep the stores clean, sell top-quality products at a low price, make people happy — that's what we're trying to do in the Hot Shoppes. If we do that, we'll succeed."[4]

These examples of purpose are just a few of the many we have heard from chief executives of highly successful businesses. The same attitudes were espoused by other successful company founders like Tom Watson of IBM, Ray Kroc of McDonald's, and Walt Disney.

It's clear that in the early days of each of these organizations, survival was the goal. Once the organization got past the "survival" milestone, however, their founders focused their attention on a broader purpose.

Where your focus is, doesn't matter as much as if you have one and if it's a sound one. Organizations that try to survive without a clear purpose tend to flounder around directionless, lose bearing, and go under.

THE VALUES VISION —
Creating a Guiding Philosophy

The second type of vision that leads to Stratgeic Focus is the Values Vision. This is a picture of the core beliefs or values that guide a company's thinking.

Following in his father's footsteps, Tom Watson, Jr., former chairman of IBM, says it best:

I firmly believe that any organization, in order to survive and achieve success, must have a sound set of beliefs on which it premises all its policies and actions.

Next, I believe that the most important single factor in corporate success is faithful adherence to those beliefs....

In other words, the basic philosophy, spirit, and drive of an organization have far more to do with its relative achievements than do technological or economic resources, organizational structure, innovation and timing.

All these things weigh heavily on success. But they are, I think, transcended by how strongly the people in the organization believe in its basic precepts and how faithfully they carry them out.[5]

IBM has operated so successfully for these many years on three simple statements of belief:

1) We believe in respect for the individual.
2) We will give the best service of any company in the world.
3) We expect superior performance from our people in all that they do.

The Matsushita Corporation in Japan listed seven "values." Employees of the organization were even required to work up presentations for fellow employees on the values. The Matsushita values are:

(1) National service through industry
(2) Fairness
(3) Harmony and cooperation
(4) Struggle for betterment
(5) Courtesy and humility
(6) Adjustment and assimilation
(7) Gratitude[6]

Perhaps the president of a small manufacturing company in the upper Mid West said it best. In describing the reason for writing a corporate creed or guiding philosophy, he said, "What I want is a statement that will guide the thinking and actions of my people. When there are two guys out on the loading dock at three o'clock in the morning debating about whether to reuse a ratty old cardboard box to ship a part to our customer, or to go back inside and get a new box, I want them to have some basis for making that decision."

That is really the essence of having a clear guiding philosophy. The words may sound like motherhood and apple pie, but the intention is to provide values that guide the thinking and actions of people on a day-to-day basis. Every company in the world has hundreds of three-o'clock in the morning loading dock decisions. Making these decisions based on a clear understanding of philosophy is better than having to go look through a twenty-eight-volume set of policy manuals.

I had the good fortune to spend several years of my career working for the Dana Corporation in Toledo. Under their visionary chairman of the board, Ren McPherson. We used to jokingly refer to Dana as the world's largest unknown company. We had $3.5 billion in sales, and no one ever heard of us. That was because we made glamorous stuff like drive shafts, universal joints and transmissions. These are products the average consumer doesn't go out shopping for, and most hope they never have to buy them.

When Peters and Waterman wrote *In Search Of Excellence*, quoting McPherson in every other chapter, suddenly Dana became a popular name in corporate America. The thing that impressed me about Peters and Waterman's work was that it was true. We were living at Dana what the writers were saying in the book. One of the things we were living was the Dana guiding philosophy.

Legend has it that soon after taking over as the chairman of Dana, McPherson called his top fifteen or eighteen people together. They were sitting in a room around a U shaped table. McPherson placed a waste can in the middle of the U. He put into it the corporate policy manual — twenty-two inches of paper. He lit the policy manual on fire and burned it to ashes.

"Gentlemen, we have no more policy manual at the Dana Corporation," said the chairman. "How are we going to run this company?"

The result of this dramatic moment was the development of a one-page statement of corporate philosophy called "The Policy Sheet." It is printed on one side of one piece of paper and includes all of the core values necessary to guide the company. Since that time, Dana has grown from $400 million to over $4.5 billion in sales. They have moved from being a centralized autocratic type of company, to a decentralized company, which provides great autonomy to their division and plant managers. Their Strategic Focus has been "Productivity Through People."

The important thing about any guiding philosophy or corporate credo is that it guides the actions and decisions of people on a day-today basis. The best example of a corporate credo that guides decisions is that of Johnson & Johnson. The maker of healthcare products was faced with a major decision when its Tylenol R pain reliever in several Chicago area drug stores was found to be laced with poison. Not knowing where the poison came from, the company decided to remove the product from the market. This was a decision that cost them millions of dollars.

James Burke, chairman of J&J, reported that the single most important factor in making the decision to pull the product from the shelves was the company's corporate credo. It begins:

> We believe our first responsibility is to the doctors, nurses and patients, to the mothers and all others who use our products and services. In meeting their needs everything we do must be of high quality.

The J&J Credo goes on to talk about responsibility to employees, community and to stockholders. But the recognition that their first responsiblity was to users of the product prompted the decision to pull the product. The decision making proved correct. A poll taken shortly after the crisis showed that ninety-three percent of the public surveyed felt that J&J had handled its responsibility well. The real test was in the marketplace. Within two years after the tragic event, Tylenol R had regained ninety percent of the market share it had lost as a result of the poisoning incident.

The Tylenol R ordeal will go down as a classic case in business history, demonstrating that a company that makes decisions based on its core values will be successful. The key is to define those core values, to communicate them to all employees, and to live by them in the decision-making process. By defining your company's core values, you also continue in the process of defining your Strategic Focus.

THE PERFORMANCE VISION
Identifying Critical Measures of Success

Of course, I am not so naive as to say that to be successful, management must ignore profits. Making a profit is a valid goal of any business, and goals are the steps you accomplish on the way to achieving your purpose. What I am saying is that if your efforts and energy are focused on a clearly defined mission, a sound purpose that considers all your organization's stakeholders, and a statement of corporate philosophy, then profits will follow. Profits are the measures of how well we do the fundamental tasks of the business.

As Stan Wells of The Barnes Group puts it, "I do think that in the end, as a public corporation, we have to be accountable for financial results. If we do all of these things right, and don't achieve superior financial results, then our whole theory is in question."

On his tape, "The Power of Purpose", David McNally reminds listeners that profits are the incentive for being in business. "The only way a business can get started is that there is a problem to be solved, a need to be met. The purpose of a business is to create and keep a customer, and profit is the requirement and reward for doing things right."[7]

Profit is not the only measure of success. Every organization should identify five to seven key indicators that show the overall picture of performance. These are what I call the CRITICAL MEASURES OF SUCCESS.

The problem with most organizations I have observed is not that they don't have measures of performance. It is that they have too many. Top executives are overwhelmed with information. They try to absorb all of the numbers, and they tend to spend too much time putting out fires when one number gets out of whack.

My favorite analogy here is the pilot of a 747. He has twenty-eight feet of dials, switches, gauges and lights on the dashboard in front of him. It's a massive management information system. But nobody can watch all of those twenty-eight feet of indicators and respond to all of them at once.

I am told that a good pilot has six or seven key dials that he looks at on a regular basis during flight. As long as all of those gauges are pointing at the appropriate numbers, the pilot knows his aircraft is on course. If one of the dials moves off, or if a red light goes on, the pilot recognizes that corrective action is necessary. That action might be a minor course correction, or it might be a major emergency procedure. In any event, the pilot has a backup system to tell him more about the problem.

The same thing is true for good sailboat skippers. They have six or seven key indicators that they look at continuously throughout their sail. Those indicators provide information for minor course corrections to get the most performance from the boat.

My very first consulting client when I started in business in 1979 was Bob Sweet, president of Creative Pultrusions. CP is the second-largest manufacturer in the U.S. of fiberglass pultrusions, with sales approaching $20 million. For the past ten years Bob and his key managers have run their company by keeping a close eye on six key numbers: sales, profit, scrap, productivity, line utilization and on-time shipments. These six numbers give such an accurate measure of company performance that every employee receives a bonus based on them. As long as these numbers keep moving in a positive direction every month, Bob and his people know that their focus on product quality and customer satisfaction is paying off.

The opposite extreme is the utility company I once worked with. They had twenty-four financial goals, many of them divided into sub-groups. Their management information system was required to process huge amounts of data, and they insisted on 100% accuracy. The result was massive reports that were always forty-five days after the close of the month. This meant that top managers didn't have a handle on what was going on in the organization. Middle managers couldn't make course corrections in their departments because by the time they got performance information, the next fiscal month was already over.

Another problem I see is that too many managers only look at the balance sheet and income statement as indicators of success. There are other critical measures that indicate a company's performance. They may be things like market share, quality, customer service, competitor performance, or even employee satisfaction.

Over the past five years, I have conducted Executive Strategy Retreats for sixty or seventy organizations. When I have them work through this question of critical measures of success, an interesting phenomenon occurs. Every group identifies "Customer Satisfaction" as one of their critical measures of success. Yet when we look at how they currently measure it, not one of them has had a system in place to measure customer satisfaction.

Every company we work with spends huge amounts of money to measure financial results. These same companies all agree that customer satisfaction is an extremely important measure of success, yet none had spent any significant amount of time, money or effort measuring it.

That is slowly changing, but it will continue to be a problem for some time. We are so accustomed to measuring short term financial results because that is where most executive compensation is based. Other critical measures of success are not tied to executive compensation, so time and money are not spent to measure them.

Comparing Japanese corporations' purposes and goals with their American counterparts, businessman and author Akio Morita says that Japanese companies are not under pressure to show profits like American companies are because Japanese shareholders prefer long-term growth and appreciation over immediate returns. "If you are nothing but profit-conscious, you cannot see the opportunities ahead," Morita says. "And where compensation is tied to profits, as it is in most American companies, very often a manager will say, why should I sacrifice my own profits today for the guy who is going to follow me in this job a few years from now?"

The key then is to have your top executive team agree on five to seven critical measures of success for the company. There should be several financial and several non-financial measures. They should indicate true long-term performance.

This concept can be carried throughout the organization. Each department or division should identify five to seven indicators of their success. This is relatively easy to do in the production department. It becomes more difficult in staff departments like legal, or human resources. But if there are no measures of success, how do you know if you are doing the right things, and doing things right?

Many organizations have management by objectives or some other type of goals-based performance management system. When you begin to look at individual objectives, you see that people are measuring their activity, not their results. As long as people are busy, and getting their tasks done, they believe they are performing well and should be compensated accordingly. The real question is, are you doing tasks that really contribute to overall corporate mission and purpose.

In so many organizations, we see people doing work that doesn't really contribute to the purpose of the business. They keep doing the task because, "We've always done it this way." Then another task is added to the job, and pretty soon you have a whole new position created that has absolutely nothing to do with the Strategic Focus of the business. We've even gone so far as to have individual managers and technical people write statement of mission and purpose for their own jobs, and tie them back to the company mission and purpose.

Measuring the right indicators at the company level and at the department and division level will help you keep your focus in focus. It will help prevent distractions and dilution of effort. That is what Strategic Focus is all about: Concentrating your actions and efforts on those few factors that will help the company gain and sustain competitive advantage in the marketplace.

THE COMPETITIVE VISION
Defining Your Unique Factor

The fourth type of vision leading to Strategic Focus is the competitive vision, sometimes called the enabling vision. That is, what do we need to focus on, and what do we need to do that will enable us to gain competitive advantage. In the next chapter, we will be discussing in detail five sources of competitive advantage. They are:

- Price
- Product
- Service

- Market Niche
- Relationships

Any one of these, or a unique combination of two or more, can be used to gain competitive advantage. The question we must answer is, which of these sources is most appropriate for our customers in the markets we serve? Where are our competitors with respect to each of these sources of competitive advantage? Which of these sources will best allow us to capitalize on our strengths?

The process I use for helping clients define their competitive vision is to discuss each of the five sources of competitive advantage. Then we talk about each one. We talk about examples of each. We talk about which competitors in our industry use each one. Then we begin to explore how our customers will respond to each one. We discuss which one or which combination we have been using so far.

As the process facilitator, I write the key ideas on cards and put them up on the storyboard. Then we use critical thinking to rearrange the ideas. We go back to the basic mission and purpose of the company. We talk about how the company was started. Often, the original competitive vision was articulated by the founder. It may or may not still be relevent.

The outcome of this series of discussions is to define what Walt Disney used to call the UNIQUE FACTOR. Disney used to say that to be successful in business, you have to be unique. You must be so unique that if people want what you have to sell, they must come to you to get it.

Once you have defined your UNIQUE FACTOR, then you must describe what your company must do to make this competitive vision become reality. Often, that comes down to mastering the basic fundamentals of the business. If you are going to compete on the basis of low price, you must be very good at running a low cost operation. If you are going to compete on product quality, you must master the art of making good products. To compete on service, smiling employees and superior customer service systems are essential. Defining your competitive vision is one more step toward clarifying your Strategic Focus.

THE FOCUS VISION
Determining How to Avoid Distraction

The fifth and final vision is the focus vision. This is the vision that helps prevent distraction and dilution of effort. One of the most important strategic decisions any company can make is to decide how to decide on future products and markets. That may sound like double talk, but deciding how to decide is an important part of the strategic thinking process.

Most start-up companies have no trouble with loss of focus. They have one product, one market and relatively few customers. As the company grows and they look for opportunities for expansion, they begin to dilute their efforts. Often the companies with the biggest problem with lack of focus are big, older companies that have grown and expanded away from their original customers and markets. They forgot what made them successful, and they turned their backs on valuable customer relationships.

One of the most interesting discussions we have in our Executive Strategy Retreats is a discussion of THE DRIVING FORCE. THE DRIVING FORCE is a concept that was developed by Ben Tregoe and John Zimmerman of Kepner & Tregoe and described in their book, *Top Management Strategy*. They define THE DRIVING FORCE as the single most important factor in determining future products and markets. They identified nine strategic areas of business. They maintain that if a company can select one of these areas as its driving force, all future decisions about products and markets will be easier.

The way I use this concept is to give a brief explanation of each of the nine strategic areas, with examples. Then I lead a discussion, forcing the group to select just one driving force. This is always an extremely interesting discussion, because it forces managers to consider some "what if" types of situations and to try to anticipate the future. One of the hardest things for them to anticipate is how they will react when a new business opportunity comes along.

The concept of THE DRIVING FORCE helps executives make consistent decisions when they consider new products and new markets. It helps them avoid the trap of trying to be all things to all people — the single biggest cause of lack of focus.

Target Your Markets

One thing we have observed that has come out of the Focus Vision discussion is a much clearer definition of target markets. Companies are much better able to define the specific groups of customers they would like to serve. By concentrating their efforts on a few specific target markets, they are able to gain better penetration of those markets.

We mentioned earlier that the biggest cause of lack of focus is the "be all things to all people" syndrome. Companies try to serve every possible customer with the broadest possible product line. Part of the reason is that top executives are reluctant to limit themselves, and possibly miss an opportunity in some new product or market.

Our observation is just the opposite. The more tightly focused a company is on its selected target markets, the more growth opportunities come along and the more successful the company is. The best place to get new product ideas is from your customers. The more you focus on a narrow group of customers, the more likely you are to develop long-term relationships. As you gain the trust and confidence of your customers and build a reputation for dependability, the more they will help you understand their needs and wants. The more you can respond to their specific needs and wants, the stronger your competitive advantage becomes.

Fives types of vision lead to Strategic Focus: The Business Vision, The Values Vision, The Performance Vision, The Competitive Vision, and The Focus Vision. Work through the creation of these five visions, and you have created the basis for focusing your company. The more tightly focused you become, the greater your ability to gain and sustain competitive advantage in the marketplace.

KEY POINTS

(1) **Strategic Focus begins with vision.**

(2) **There are Five Types of Strategic Vision: The Business Vision, The Values Vision, The Performance Vision, The Competitive Vision, and The Focus Vision.**

(3) **Mission defines What business you are in. Purpose defines Why you are in that business.**

(4) **Your Guiding Philosophy should help guide the actions and decisions of all of your people.**

(5) **The Critical Measures of Success tell you that you are doing the right things for your customers, and doing things right.**

(6) **To gain and sustain competitive advantage in the marketplace, you must be unique. Define your Unique Factor.**

(7) **The concept of the DRIVING FORCE will help you make decisions about future products and markets.**

(8) **Select target markets where you can focus your energy and effort.**

NOTES:

[1] Ted Levitt, *The Marketing Imagination* (New York: The Free Press, 1986) p. 7.

[2] Ibid, p. 9.

[3] Robert O'Brien, *Marriott* (Salt Lake City, Utah: Deseret Book Co., 1978) p. 136.

[4] Ibid, p. 173.

[5] Thomas J. Watson, Jr., *A Business and Its Beliefs* (New York: McGraw-Hill, 1963) p. 3. (as quoted in Steiner, Strategic Planning, p. 151.)

[6] David A. Aaker, *Strategic Market Management* (New York: John Wiley & Sons) p. 149

[7] David McNally, Tape: "The Power of Purpose" (Shorewood, MN: Trans-Form Corp., 1987)

CHAPTER FOUR

How to Focus on Your Competitive Advantage

PURPOSE: *To present five differentials a company can use for focusing competitive advantage and to explain how you can select the one that seems to be your greatest strength.*

To be all things to all people is impossible. To be competitive, you must have a differential advantage — you have to focus on what you can do better than any of your competitors.

Webster's New Collegiate Dictionary defines the word differential as "distinguishing or making a distinction between," and advantage as "superiority of position or condition, a benefit resulting from some course of action, or a factor or circumstance of benefit to its possessor." All those attributes fit into our understanding of the term differential advantage as we use it here. For our purposes, let's define a differential advantage as that unique element that causes your targeted customers to accept your products or services over all others on the market.

The perceived value of your product or service is directly related to how many people are using it. Diamonds have tremendous value because of their rarity. You can find rocks on roads all across the country, so they have much less perceived value than do diamonds. When we talk about perceived value, we're talking about differential advantage.

Successful organizations plan and design for that differential advantage. Before they will buy into your organization, stakeholders want to know that you offer that edge over your competitors.

The purpose of this chapter is to explain five sources a business might adopt to gain and sustain a competitive advantage. We'll include examples of organizations that were successful in their attempts to accomplish that feat in their field; examples of some companies that grabbed, but were unable to hold onto an advantage; and some "good ideas" that simply never got off the ground. My goal here is to stimulate your thinking and to help you determine which of the five sources of competitive advantage — or which combinations of them — will be most satisfactory for your organization.

The sources we will be discussing in this chapter are:

    (1) Low price
    (2) Product uniqueness
    (3) Service differentiation
    (4) Narrow market focus
    (5) Relationships

Let's understand at the start that you cannot take advantage of them all. You can combine compatible features like narrow market focus and product or service differentiation, and you could conceivably combine narrow market focus and relationships or differentiation and relationships. But you can't have the lowest price and product differentiation. It would be all but impossible to have the lowest price and best product quality. And you can't successfully have the lowest price and narrow market focus. Low price demands wide market and high volume.

LOW PRICE

Low price is a focus that many organizations have used in their attempt to gain more sales. The premise is simple: lower the price, and people will buy more of your products. In fact some organizations have been very successful by being the low-priced competitor early in the development of an industry or product line. The classic examples are in the retailing industry.

The Joseph B. Dahlkemper Company, mentioned earlier, was a forerunner of today's catalog showroom industry. This is an industry that was built on the basis of low price. Joe and Lois Dahlkemper heard about the idea of selling merchandise to individuals at wholesale prices. They decided to set up a merchandise club. They charged a small membership fee that entitled their "members" to come into their warehouse and buy direct.

The early operation was a no-frills, plain-brown-cardboard-box packaged product with primary sales coming from the catalog. Customers would come into the warehouse, pick the desired item out of a catalog, and place an order; the merchandise would be retrieved from the back of the warehouse and handed over.

The Dahlkempers lined up with Harold Roitenberg of Minneapolis, who headed a company called Creative Merchandising. Together they formed a group to share in the costs of producing their catalogs. This became the basis for today's catalog production companies.

This system worked well for many years. However, as the companies became more sophisticated, they set up merchandise display areas, fixed up their showrooms, and hired sales counselors. By the late 1970's they had shifted their strategy. According to Mary Ellen Razanauskas, vice president of Human Resources at Dahlkempers, "We chose to shift our focus. In surveying our customers we discovered that, when given a choice of the most important reasons for shopping at a certain store, eighty percent selected quality and service over price. Price was and still is important, but we no longer have to be the lowest price to compete."

The difficulty is that low price is difficult to sustain. You can buy business today by lowering your price, but someone will always come along and sell the same or similar product at a lower price.

Sam Walton's Wal-Mart stores, located primarily in the South and East, appear to have captured a top slot in the discount store group. Wal-Mart has successfully maintained a low-price position for an extended period of time, but price is not the only factor that has enabled the organization to hold its slot. Walton's stores have combined relatively high quality products, excellent merchandising on the floor, and customer service with their attractive prices.

Sam Walton, by the way, was identified in *Forbes Magazine* as the wealthiest man in America in 1989.

Another example of low price combined with other factors comes from my home town of Lock Haven, Pennsylvania. William T. Piper, often referred to as the "Henry Ford of Aviation," founded Piper Aircraft there.

I got a chance to see Piper's success first hand as I grew up with Mr. Piper's grandsons during the company's heyday. Mr. Piper realized the potential of the aircraft industry and took as his mission the design and building of inexpensive airplanes. In a burst of insight and foresight, he wanted not only an inexpensive airplane, but he also decreed that his planes must be easy to fly. The company's target market was the person who gave flying lessons. As a result of focusing their original effort, the Piper Aircraft Corporation was very successful. The company prospered until it was bought out by a conglomerate.

PRODUCT UNIQUENESS

A second source of competitive advantage, product differentiation, exists when an organization is able to develop a product or service and position it in the minds of customers as significantly different from other products or services. The differentiation may come from a perception of superior quality or superior value, or it may be a case of a company being able to capitalize on the emotional buying habits of customers.

Remember we said earlier that perception may be the most important word in the commercial world. Customers value products and services proportionate to their perception of each commodity's ability to fill their needs.

Picture a scenario in which a customer is standing in a store looking at television sets. He sees two that he likes. One of them is priced $150 higher than the other. In most stores, if you ask the clerk what the difference in the two sets is, he or she will answer, "$150." What the customer wants to know is, "What is there about set A that would make me willing to pay $150 more for it than for set B?"

There are probably a number of pens on the market that perform fully as well as a Cross pen, but how many high school graduates proudly announce that they received a Scripto pen-and-pencil set from Uncle Homer and Aunt Carrie? And when a young executive purchases a quality pen to carry in a shirt pocket, it's a Cross pen, not a Pentel. Cross, a Connecticut-based company, has been able to create a classic, slim, gold or silver pen-and-pencil set that is perceived to be superior to other ball point pens. The Parker Company was able to do the same thing a few decades ago with fountain pens, but they did not anticipate and corner the market when ball point instruments were developed.

Now, designer jeans are a different matter. Most any customer is willing to pay twice the average price of a pair of blue jeans for a pair with the right name sewn in. Jordache took a basic commodity-type product from the cornfield to the cocktail party merely by stitching his name on the back pocket.

Reebok shoes were to the late '80s what US Keds were to the late '60s. Our parents would have balked at paying $40 to $80 for a pair of gym shoes, but television commercials, their peers, and professional athletes convinced children of the '80s that they would have to hide their feet under the chair if they were clad in anything other than untied, flopping Reeboks.

Our children aren't the only ones who are swayed by company positioning. Homeowners continue to pay as high as $150 price premiums for Maytag clotheswashers and Kitchen Aid dishwashers because they are "the top of the line."

It's all perception.

An attempt at product differentiation based on quality has failed, however, for a struggling entrepreneur in South Carolina.

Max Watson builds woodstoves. His Biltmore Stove is undoubtedly the finest on the market. It's constructed of double-thick metal with hand-welded joints. Watson included catalytic converters on his stoves long before anyone else realized their importance. He tests under pressure for leakage and air control. With recent fuel crunches in this country, Watson has a sure winner, right? Wrong.

Buckstove can make and sell stoves at retail for a little more than half what Biltmores go for — wholesale. People buy woodstoves in an economy move, and it doesn't make sense to buy a $1500 stove because you can't afford to pay high utility bills.

Watson is in a situation where the perceived value of his product is not commensurate with the quality that he is trying to maintain. His ethic is: "I will make the finest stove that I can possibly make." Ethics are fine if you can afford them, but who cares if he makes the finest stove that money can buy, if the customer doesn't perceive the added value?

The Charles Revson Revlon nail polish story is an early example of successful product differentiation. Revson's approach was that nail polish was a fashion accessory, not a mere beauty aid, and that women should use different shades to suit different outfits, different moods and different occasions. This thought process enticed women to buy several bottles of the compound for their dressers and broadened the market dramatically.

Revson made a conscious decision not to compete on price, but on quality. He made it clear that he wasn't selling the fact that his polish was made of pigment and completely covered the nails or that his price was better than his competitors. He was selling glamour, attention and excitement.[1] Clairol's "Blondes have more fun" line accomplishes the same purpose. It's the idea that sells the product.

Revson understood the difference between a differentiated product and a commodity. It's the difference between Jordache and Levi jeans. Both have brand names, but one goes with a Mercedes, the other with a tractor.

SERVICE DIFFERENTIATION

Product differentiation applies to services as readily as it does to ball point pens and blue jeans.

In the airline industry, for instance, the product relates to how the passenger gets from point A to point B. The product includes reservations, ticketing, boarding, baggage handling, inflight attention, exiting the plane, and all the other factors involved in getting from here to there. As Ted Levitt said in *The Marketing Imagination*, the important thing to know about differentiating intangible products is that customers don't usually know what they are getting until they don't.[2]

Product differentiation is difficult in a service business, because the customer, as Levitt points out, may be aware of failure or dissatisfaction and may not be aware of success or satisfaction. For example, if an airline passenger gets from A to B on time with relatively little hassle, he or she says, "That's fine. That's what I expected. That's what I paid for." But if the plane is late or baggage is lost, a passenger becomes dissatisfied — and that may be describing the reaction mildly.

Customers for regularly delivered and consumed intangible products must be constantly reminded of what they're getting. The wife of one of our clients, a Chrysler-Plymouth dealer, goes to the business each morning and gets a list of customers whose cars were serviced the day before. She calls a random selection of those customers to find out how the work was handled and to remind them of the dealership's desire to provide superior service.

DIFFERENTIATING THROUGH SERVICE MEANS MORE THAN JUST BEING NICE

I distinguish between intangible products and service. The intangible product is the way in which an airplane gets a passenger from A to B. Service is the way in which the airline deals with the customer in the process.

There are a number of well-known companies that have gained and sustained a significant competitive advantage through the way they provide service. The classic example of differentiation through service is International Business Machines Corp. One of IBM's three guiding philosophy statements says, "We will give the best service of any company in the world." IBM lives up to that expectation. They are known worldwide for going out of their way to solve a customer's problem.

If you study IBM's record over the last fifty years or so, you'll realize that the company has not always been the technological leader. Oh, they've made some new product announcements and breakthroughs, but generally, they have been second in. For example, IBM followed the likes of Apple into the personal computer business. You will also notice that IBM products are not as closely tailored to a specific application as some other company's lines and that IBM's contribution may be more expensive to the purchaser than competing brands.

As Buck Rodgers, former vice president for marketing for the business machine giant, said in his book, *The IBM Way*, "You should assume your competition also has a good product and that you must offer something extra."[3] IBM's "something extra" is unmatched service. When a piece of their equipment breaks, IBM comes to fix it. As someone once said, "They're the only computer company that answers their telephone." It's this high-level commitment to keeping their equipment running that has gained the company a substantial competitive advantage. Rodgers says the company considers selling and servicing to be synonymous.[4]

In his book, *Managing to Keep the Customer*, Robert Desatnick said he expected the last two decades of the twentieth century to be referred to as the era of customer sovereignty. "The business organizations that will succeed are those that recognize today's customer revolution and are fully prepared to meet the challenge at the highest standards of service."[5]

An example of superior service from my days with Joy Manufacturing comes to mind. The company had just installed the first 12CM coal miner in a mine in southwestern Pennsylvania. My task was to go in with a crew to videotape the prototype in operation.

We arrived at the mine and went underground to find the service engineer who had installed the equipment still there. An electrical problem on the machine had already kept the engineer underground for eight hours.

The engineer's cap lamp went dead. He borrowed another light and continued working. Of course, the problem meant we couldn't take any film of the machine in operation, so we all stood around watching. When after several more hours the installer still could not get the bugs out, he telephoned the chief research and development engineer at the plant, 125 miles away. The men could not trouble shoot satisfactorily by telephone, so the engineer made the three-hour drive to the mine, came underground, found the problem, got the machine up and running, drove the return 125 miles and finished his shift in Joy's engineering department. Now that's commitment to service.

McDonald's Restaurants rival IBM in the "service award of the century" competition. The organization's focus on the customer and attention to the McDonald's philosophy of quality, service, cleanliness and value has enabled them to remain the leader in the fast-food industry for many years. One of their franchisees, however, has out-McDonalded McDonald's in creating value for customers.

Angelo Lencioni and Cathy Connelly run one of the ten busiest McDonald's in the world at North Clark Street in Chicago. They hold weekly sock hops and vintage car shows during the summer months and hire a Santa, Mrs. Claus and an elf to join customers during the Christmas season. Their decor includes $1 million in pinball machines, a Thunderbird convertible and such rock-n-roll paraphernalia as life-sized plaster casts of the Beatles.

The Clark Street Store charges a little more than most stores for their products, but they have no problem staying busy. More than 300,000 customers patronize the business monthly, spending an average of $3 each. "I want the customer who spends $1.78 on a Big Mac to leave with $2 of value," Lencioni said of his store's service.[6]

NARROW MARKET FOCUS

Our fourth source of competitive advantage is having an

organization focus its products or services on a very narrow, relatively small market. The idea in focusing narrowly is that you will be able to serve a particular niche more effectively than will companies that compete on a broader scale.

The Mercedes-Benz organization has successfully focused on a narrow market. The organization provides a product that is perceived to be of extremely high quality and delivered with a high level of service to a relatively small market niche made up of affluent people who are willing and able to spend $50,000 to $100,000 for an automobile.

Neiman-Marcus targets the same market. The department store stocks only quality products and offers a high level of service at a premium price to a narrow, up-scale market.

A narrow market can be successfully achieved for any product that fills a desire or a need, not just top quality and service for the affluent.

It took courage for The W.S. Wells and Son Cannery in Wilton, Maine, to halt their general canning production and focus on preserving only gourmet greens. Butch Wells, son of the company founder, watched fifteen canneries in his area go out of business in a thirty-year period and knew he had to take action. Instead of beans and tomatoes, Wells and Son is the only company in the United States to concentrate a commercial production on dandelion and beet greens and fiddle heads, the curled-up tops of the ostrich fern.

Wells found a need that was not being met and created a way to meet it. "It's not that everybody loves greens, but those who do can't seem to get enough of them," he said.

Bookseller Carol Brener also found a tight niche into which she could slip successfully. More than 20,000 crime novels, spy stories and thrillers line the shelves of Murder Ink, Brener's Manhattan book store. The owner gives away gun-shaped book-marks and publishes a store newsletter. She survives on $3.50 sales, only occasionally coming across a collector's edition in her mostly used books.

"I have a Macy's mentality," Brener said. "I'd rather sell 100 books at $5 each than one at $500."[7]

Focusing can also go big time if you get the right product at the right place and time. Toys 'R' Us did that.

Toys'R'Us founder, Charles Lazarus, keeps a tight rein on business in his more than 300 stores across the country. Don't go to Toys 'R' Us if you're looking for tools. Lazarus stocks only toys and associated items and sells them year round at low prices; and he doesn't provide wide aisles, attractive displays, and service on the sales floor. He demands of his suppliers that their products be packaged in sturdy boxes printed on all six sides with identification and operating instructions.

With his tight focus, the master toy salesman's take of the toy market is twenty-five percent and climbing. Parents, who formerly sent their children to the department store toy section to play while they browsed in housewares, now make a list, go to the Toys'R'Us supermarket, get the goods, and go.

Sidney Biddle Barrows, the reknowned Mayflower Madam of the mid-'80s, exhibited an acute mind for the business and financial side of her enterprise. Although your organization might not be interested in competing in Barrows' "escort service" market, you'll find she followed a pretty good business strategy. She was doing exceptionally well, providing a much sought after service, until tracked down by the long arm of the law. I share some of her strategy with you, because they are good rules of thumb; of course, with tongue-in-cheek.

(1) Provide a dramatic alternative to what's available in your field.

(2) No matter what business you are in, get to know your customer and offer the kind of merchandise he or she will like.

(3) Find good people and pay them what they're worth.

(4) Let your employees know that you recognize and value their hard work.

(5) A store is nothing more than an aggregate of customers. Pay close attention to what they want.

RELATIONSHIPS
Sometimes, It's Who You Know

The fifth source of competitive advantage focuses on relationships. The basic strategy in developing business based on relationships usually requires the principal officers of an organization to spend a great deal of time making personal contacts with potential customers and referral sources.

Typically, professional service firms such as consultants, public accountants, attorneys and physicians have built highly successful businesses based on relationships. Once a relationship is established, the customer or client finds changing to a competing firm extremely difficult. A situation develops where, all things being equal, people would rather do business with a friend.

And, in many instances, evidence shows that even with all things being unequal, people will still do business with a friend. This attitude is particularly true if the relationship is created in such a way as to minimizes risk or fear to a customer.

A couple of examples of successful focus based on relationships come from my files. Ruthanne Nerlich, executive director of Visiting Nurse Association of Venango County, has been able to corner and keep almost 100% of the home health care market share for more than fifteen years in Venango County, Pennsylvania.

Growth and changes in the medical delivery system in the early 1980s led many health professionals to focus on in-home care. Changes in government reimbursement policies indicated that a lucrative market was developing across the country, and people rushed to get a portion of the prize. The industry became highly competitive.

Nerlich, a long-time health professional in the area, was able to capitalize on an established rapport with hospitals, physicians and other health-delivery organizations in the area to build and sustain a competitive advantage. As a result of her relationships with referral groups, Nerlich has been able to construct a sound financial position for her agency and to prevent private companies and hospitals alike from getting a toehold in the field.

Another individual who has been successful in building a

business based on relationships is Californian Ann Boe. Boe is a public speaker and consultant who specializes in a concept called networking. Her basic premise is that individuals will be more successful if they devote time and energy to building a network of people on whom they can depend for various kinds of help. Networks are mutually supportive. Established relationships provide those networks.

To gain knowledge about networking, Boe developed her own supportive network, on which she has, in turn, built a thriving public-speaking business. For several years, 100% of her engagements have come from repeat business and referrals. Her only marketing function is to meet people and build relationships.

The relationship strategy is probably not one that is appropriate for major manufacturing companies or multi-channel service businesses, but the strategy holds high potential for personal service firms.

SOME COMBINATIONS
JUST GO WELL TOGETHER

We've talked about the five sources of competitive advantage and given you some examples of each. We realize, however, that a few organizations use only a single Strategic Focus to gain competitive advantage. In most successful companies, we see what we might call some classic combinations.

Caterpillar Tractor provides one such classic combination. Caterpillar has combined a high-quality product, a focus on twenty-four-hour parts service anywhere in the world, and the relationships of an extensive dealer network. I call this combination "reliability."

Most customers are not as interested in a product's features or function as they are concerned with what the product will do for them. Caterpillar recognized that if a product is broken down, it can't do anything for its owner. As a result of this insight, the company has built a highly competitive, worldwide business based on the combination of high quality, effective service and an extensive dealer network to build relationships with key customers.

We've already mentioned McDonald's constant focus on the customer and their guiding philosophy of quality, service, cleanliness and value. The key to McDonald's success, however, has been consistency. Whatever the company does, it does the same way every time, everywhere it operates. A Big Mac tastes the same in Oil City, Pennsylvania, as it does in New York, Chicago or Toronto.

The secret to market success is to investigate and understand the potential sources of competitive advantage for your organization and to develop a combination that enables you to sustain a strong position over a long period of time.

KEY POINTS

(1) **To be competitive, you must focus on what you can do better than any of your competitors.**

(2) **The five sources of competitive advantage are:**
  (A) **Low price**
  (B) **Product uniqueness**
  (C) **Service differentiation**
  (D) **Narrow market focus**
  (E) **Relationships**

(3) **Usually an organization already has a differential advantage, and it's simply a matter of finding it, sharpening it and cashing in on it, as opposed to creating it.**

(4) **Customers value products and services proportionate to their perception of that commodity's ability to fill their needs.**

(5) **Product differentiation applies to services as readily as it does to a product.**

(6) **Customers for regularly delivered and consumed intangible products must be constantly reminded of what they're getting.**

NOTES:

[1] Andrew Tobias, *Fire and Ice*, (New York: Quill, 1983), p. 107-108.

[2] Theodore Levitt, *The Marketing Imagination* (New York: The Free Press, 1986), p. 105.

[3] Buck Rodgers, *The IBM Way* (New York: Harper & Row, 1986) p. 137.

[4] Ibid. p. 163.

[5] Robert L. Desatnick, *Managing to Keep the Customer* (San Francisco: Jossey-Bass Publishers, 1987) p. 1.

[6] *USA Today*, Dec. 14, 1987, sec. B, p. 4.

[7] *USA Today*, July 17, 1987, sec. B, p. 4.

CHAPTER FIVE

How to Position Yourself
for Your Best
Strategic Advantage

PURPOSE: *To show how positioning can enable you to establish and maintain a competitive advantage in today's global marketplace.*

Technically speaking, positioning means creating the right perceptions within the minds of your stakeholders, your targeted audience. It is the task of presenting who you are and what you do — to the right people, in the right way. In their definitive book on positioning, Al Ries and Jack Trout say that effective positioning "takes into consideration not only a company's own strengths and weaknesses, but those of its competitors as well."[1]

"We do chicken right" is Kentucky Fried Chicken's positioning statement to the mass market. Once Col. Sanders got the business rolling, that "best in the flock" focus existed; but when Sanders retired from active participation, the organization began to flounder, trade dropped off, and growth slackened. Sanders' successors wanted to become the supermarket of the fast foods business. They started adding all kinds of other items to the menu.

Finally, someone in the organization saw the light and the

word went forth: "Hey, wait a minute. Our differential advantage is chicken. Let's get back to what we do best."

An advantage usually exists. The key to Strategic Focus is finding and exploiting your greatest and most marketable advantage.

Once your organization has selected a focus of competitive advantage or a classic combination of competitive features, the next step is to position yourself well in the minds of your customers. Remember that perception is the key word. The only thing that matters is how the customer sees you.

To position yourself well in the minds of your customers, you need to consider the following questions:

(1) How do we want the customer to see our product, service or company?

(2) How does the customer now see our product, our service or our company?

(3) What must we do to insure that the customer views us the way we want to be viewed?

An exercise you might use to determine your current position in the mind of your stakeholders and customers is to ask: "If you were going to describe our company and our product to a close friend, what would you say?"

If the responses to your query match your desired description, if they come close to describing your purpose, you have positioned your company in a way that will enable you to sustain your selected competitive advantage. If you get descriptions dramatically different from your own concepts of who you are and what you are about, you have a great deal of work to do. It's time to think through a battle plan, come up with a strategy to get you from where you are to where you want to be. And while you are developing your strategy, keep in mind that it takes far less energy — less expense, fewer resources — to increase your market share than it takes to increase the size of your market. So be prepared for some fierce competition from the other organizations who are fighting to hold their position or to gain new ground.

There Are Limits to What You Can Accomplish

The whole concept of market share is that, realistically, the market for a particular product or service has limits in size. The easiest and most productive way to market your product is to find the people who are your most logical and likely customers, because they are the ones who are easiest to sell to.

If you are operating a hospital, for instance, you want to gear up for sick folks. Hospital administrators know that a certain percentage of people in the area will need hospitalization. The administrators set goals and make plans with those figures in mind. They don't go out and try to make people sick so that they will have to use their services.

Adding a new hospital in an area does not increase the market share; it simply divides the potential share into smaller portions. In other words, the market is divided by the number of competitors. If you have a twenty percent share of a particular market and increase that share to twenty-two percent, you have to take that new two percent away from somebody else.

That's why strategic thinking is so crucial in the marketplace. That's why when people sit back and criticize television networks for playing the ratings game, they are dreaming. In the real world, any television network that hopes to survive is going to have to play the ratings game, and those who play it best will win. The show that captures the largest audience during a particular hour will also capture the largest amount of advertising.

The concept is like a bunch of little boys playing "keepers" with marbles on the school ground:

Each child starts with a cache of marbles. The market share of marbles is basically stable. A new kid would have to enroll in the school or an established player would have to get a new sack of marbles for a birthday or at Christmas to alter the basic market share.

The system is a continual swapping of the same marbles back and forth. The less adept players lose their marbles to the better players.

Most of the organizations we consult with on positioning have already determined what their niche is — who they are and what their markets are. We are talking with them about how to best present themselves to gain an increased share of their potential market. We help them arrive at strategies to take full advantage of all the resources they have available to increase their competitive edge.

Their goal is to utilize their resources in a way that customers find more desirable than anything available from competitors. They want to draw up a battle plan to take full advantage of employee and community relationships, capital investment and productivity. The market element is the key element, but it's not the total picture. Achieving a desired position requires attention to the broad spectrum, assessing where you are, where you want to be and what it will take to get there.

In addition to those three points, your strategic plan will need to include a study of where the market is going and what you can do to gain a competitive edge in that market. You will need to consider such questions as:

(1) Will my product be attractive in the market? Do I offer something that is clearly distinguishable from or superior to my competitors' products?

(2) Can I produce at a capacity that will enable me to offer competitive prices?

(3) Can I develop a delivery system that will enable me to serve the customer in ways that are superior to my competition?

(4) Do I have a marketing strategy that will enable me to present and sell my product in the market-place?

(5) What are my competitors likely to do in response to my shift in Strategic Focus?

It All Depends on Where You Are Now

Your approach to planning an action strategy will, of course, depend on your present position. Before you can develop an effective strategy, you need to assess where you are in relation to your competitors by determining what market share you currently hold. If you are already dominant in the market and are trying to maintain that dominance, there are certain moves to take to secure your position. If you are number two or three and are trying to gain in market share, you need a different strategy.

Probably the best book we have today on Strategic Focus and management was written four centuries before the birth of Jesus. Chinese General Sun Tzu's *The Art of War*[2] offers timeless tips on strategy, tactics and psychology that today's executives would be well advised to heed.

Commenting on the order of battle, Sun Tzu gave us some good advice for strategic planning:

> What is of supreme importance is to attack the enemy's strategy.

> When he concentrates, prepare against him; where he is strong, avoid him.

> As water shapes its flow in accordance with the ground, so an army manages its victory in accordance with the situation of the enemy.

> Those skilled at making the enemy move do so by creating a situation to which he must conform.

Your strategies will be determined by your size and position and that of your competitors. The key issue is: Why would potential customers choose you over your competitors?

We can assume, for example, that someone who is in the market for a new car is going to buy an automobile. So if you are a dealer, your strategic planning must determine why that person would buy an automobile from one dealer rather than from another and what you can do to see that he or she buys from you rather than from your competitor.

Also, you need a plan of action that will translate your market strategy into tangible terms to quickly and effectively entrench your dealership in the mind of that potential car buyer.

For instance, if you are what these days is commonly called a "mega-dealer," you might talk about how you sell more cars per day than anybody in your area. The benefit to the customer in such circumstances, of course, is that you can sell at much cheaper prices than your competitors because you buy in such large volume.

If, on the other hand, you are a small dealer, your marketing approach might be that you sell in small volume and consequently can offer the personal touch both in sales and in service.

When You Lead the Pack, You Can Play Defensively

According to top positioning experts, only the individual or organization who holds the dominant position in the marketplace can afford to act defensively.

Courageous defensive strategy, they say, would be to attack yourself. The fried chicken place that establishes a fast-order seafood business on an adjoining lot attacks itself, but it also captures a fresh market share. Families who are split between whether they will eat chicken or fish do not have to choose, they can drive into one parking lot and each family member can take advantage of the preferred menu. Placing the competing businesses in adjacent locations will probably have a synergistic affect. Each will attract individual customers and the combination will attract still another market that increases the individual store's business.

A cannery that markets peas under a leading label attacks itself by also producing a generic, no-label line, but it will probably take more of a lower-priced competitor's customers than it will of its own.

Attacking yourself can be a strong blocking move against a competitor who attempts to steal your market share with a similar product or a cheaper price advantage.

A small independent seafood company can turn the tables on the chicken fast food giant, however, by establishing a competing store adjacent to the better-known business. Instead of the chicken place sharing its business with itself and increasing traffic from new customers drawn by its own competing partner, it will feel its business drained by the enemy next door.

If You're Looking to Climb, You'll Need a Strong Offense

If you face an entrenched foe, you will have to go on the offensive to gain any ground. Tzu recommended finding a weakness in the leader's strength and attacking at that point.

Anciently, the skillful warriors first made themselves invincible and awaited the enemy's moment of vulnerability.

Invincibility depends on one's self; the enemy's vulnerability on him. It follows that those skilled in war can make themselves invincible but cannot cause an enemy to be certainly vulnerable.

Therefore it is said that one may know how to win, but cannot necessarily do so.

Invincibility lies in the defense; the possibility of victory in the attack.

Remember the Avis Rent-a-Car strategy. Admitting that they were Number Two, the organization declared "We're Number Two, We Try Harder" in order to get business. Burger King took advantage of increased national concern over health a few years ago, and offered flame-broiled burgers to combat McDonald's stranglehold on the fast-food lane. Burger King employees say they don't mind handing customers a Whopper when they come in and ask for a Big Mac. McDonald's management, on the other hand, would probably get a little shaky in their leading position if too many of their patrons asked for Whoppers.

Although he didn't call it that, Sun Tzu even had a strategy for blindsiding the competition and moving into unbroken ground.

Speed is the essence. Take advantage of the enemy's unpreparedness; travel by unexpected routes and strike him where he has taken no precautions.

Those skilled in war bring the enemy to the field of battle and are not brought there by him.

Land's polaroid camera moved in on Eastman Kodak territory, dealing a heavy blow that took years for Eastman to over-come. And when Eastman did release a competing product, the strategy was poorly thought out. The new self-developing camera lacked the quality that customers had come to expect of Land products, and the subsequent patent-infringement battle in the courts forced the newer item into oblivion. The presiding judge in the case ruled that customers who had bought the cameras could get their money back from Kodak.

If you're a comer, the best idea is to study the market and find yourself a product and a position that is unique and narrow enough to defend, then be prepared to fight for it or to take off in a new direction if necessary.

Bigg's, a new chain which is moving into the U.S., is called a hypermarket. Already established in Europe and South America, hypermarkets are the newest version of the old country store — a general mercantile. Before the days of good roads and fast cars, people shopped primarily in their own community, and the merchant sold everything from crackers to cloth to claw hammers. The hypermarkets, which are moving in on the market shares of a number of different types of businesses, are as big as several football fields, have forty to eighty check-out lines, and sell anything from rolls to ready-made garments to refrigerators. Their competitive advantage is to cater to busy people who do not have time to shop several locations for a variety of items. Shoppers can find anything they want under one roof.

Kroger is one of the established supermarkets that has been hard hit by the hypermarkets. In response, it has opened its own Welcome stores, which combine groceries, a deli, a drug store and cosmetic counters at a single site.

Supermarket consultant, Willard Bishop, says the level of general merchandise sales will determine the success of the hypermarket concept. The higher mark-up available in other areas will allow cuts in the cost of food items.[3]

Don't Ever Admit to Being Top Dog

We've all heard politicians say they'd rather be down in the polls; that they work harder if they're the underdog and that they also garner a sympathy vote from being in the loser position.

It's the same in sports. A team of players that take the field feeling cocky about beating their opponent is apt to lack the drive, the grit-your-teeth-and-go-after-them attitude that it takes to win. And like in the Old West, everybody is out to challenge the fastest gun in town.

Above all, if you are top dog, don't let anybody outside your organization know how you got there. The Colonel said, "We do chicken right," but he didn't say how he did it. The secret recipe was kept locked away in the safe.

Today's business community is no longer the country merchant competing with the folks in town the hardware store in one end of town competing with one in the other end or even large organizations on one coast competing with those on the opposite side of the country. We're all competing in a continually changing global market.

Until a few years ago, there were only a few suppliers of basic goods in the world marketplace and it was easy for us to dominate. Now, almost every little country in the world is coming on line with all kinds of production capacity. And anything these small countries do, in terms of exports, improves their economy.

We're losing our competitive advantage because we've shared our technical knowledge with developing countries. Technologies like that of the video cassette recorder, which was developed in the United States twenty or so years ago, are escaping us.

In a move to gain competitive advantage, the company that developed the VCR technology taught the Japanese how to do it, anticipating that they could produce the machines for us more economically than we could. Suddenly, the American developer found itself competing with every electronics manufacturer in Japan, because the government there took the technology and financed research to develop the VCR much faster than this one American company could. Now, no VCRs are manufactured in the U.S.

The same thing happened with photo copiers except in the case of Xerox. To try to gain a competitive edge on Xerox, the

Savin copier people gave the technology to a Japanese firm, and within a short period of time, dozens of Japanese companies were making copiers based on the same principles and technology.

So far, our foreign competitors have out-strategized us. We create ideas and technology — the expensive part of the product development process — and they bring them to market. The income is in the production and marketing, of course. We've been fools.

In the automobile industry, however, what worked for the goose is now working for the gander. The Japanese quickly saturated the world market with automobiles built more cheaply than our industry could produce them. Now they are struggling to keep making gains because Korea and Yugoslavia moved in strongly with their Hyundai and Yugo respectively.

The experts say, "No matter how successful you become, never act like the leader." The little guy in the competitive-marketing war will be able to say, "In America anything is possible," only as long as he can find a need to fill and doesn't tell all he knows.

KEY POINTS

(1) Positioning is a way of creating the right perceptions in the minds of your stakeholders.

(2) The key to Strategic Focus is finding and exploiting your greatest and most marketable advantage.

(3) It's easier to increase market share than it is to increase market size.

(4) A strategic plan should include:

    (A) A study of where the market is going and what it will take to gain a competitive edge in the market.

    (B) An analysis of where you are in relation to your competitors — what market share you currently hold.

(5) Your strategies will be determined by your size and position and that of your competitors.

(6) **When you lead the pack, you can play defensively.**

(7) **Attacking yourself can be a strong blocking move against a competitor who attempts to steal your market share.**

(8) **If you face an entrenched foe, you must go on offensive to gain ground.**

(9) **If you're top dog, don't let anyone know how you got there.**

NOTES:

[1] Al Ries and Jack Trout, *Positioning: The Battle for Your Mind* (New York: McGraw-Hill Book Co., 1981), p. 29.

[2] Sun Tzu, *The Art of War*, translated by Samuel B. Griffin (London: Oxford University Press, 1963). Excerpted in Success Magazine, Sept., 1988, pp. 56-7.

[3] Martha T. Moore, *USA Today*.

CHAPTER SIX

How to Sharpen Your Focus

PURPOSE: *To give readers some "hands-on" techniques they can use to help determine the best focus for their organization and to explain how they can mobilize their people in the search for focus.*

Strategic Focus does not come automatically; nor is it permanent. It must be pursued vigorously until it is razor sharp, then resharpened constantly.

We can look at the process for discovering focus from two angles: Some organizations inherit a guiding purpose from their founder, while others create an effective focus through careful analysis of their reason for existence.

The easiest and often the best way to establish a focus is to adopt the philosophy of your founder. Our studies of many highly successful organizations demonstrate that there was a founder with a clear vision for the organization and the ability to translate that vision into a guiding philosophy.

We could list many examples of successful companies that have adopted their founder's philosophy, but several organizations stand out.

A Gift from The Founder

Tom Watson, Sr., founder of IBM, espoused a three-fold philosophy that was common in America during the time he founded the company. The focus worked for the organization in its early days and has continued to keep it strong for years.

It's the second statement, "Give the best service of any company in the world," that has enabled IBM to gain and sustain a competitive advantage in the market- place.

Ray Kroc, founder of McDonald's Corporation, also was able to articulate a clear, simple philosophy that provided focus for his company and all of its people. Kroc focused his employee's attention on the initials QSCV, which stand for quality, service, cleanliness and value.

Those words have meaning for anyone and are concepts to which almost anybody will pay lip service. McDonald's, however, has been able to clearly define each of the terms and to back each concept a complete training program and a prototype for its franchise operations so that every McDonald's restaurant in the world demonstrates the focus — quality, service, cleanliness and value.

C.E. Woolman, founder of Delta Airlines, articulated three ideals that became the focal point in guiding philosophy for the successful company:

(1) Treat employees like members of the family.

(2) Maintain strict consistency.

(3) Thoroughly plan facilities and equipment.

By putting these three rules into action, Delta has been able to remain one of the most successful airlines in the world, with high levels of customer and employee satisfaction. The employee-satisfaction factor was demonstrated when, during the early '80s recession, Delta employees went together and purchased a much-needed new jet as a Christmas present for the company.

James O. McKinsey, founder of McKinsey and Company, one of the world's foremost management and consulting firms, listed three goals that have guided the firm's focus. McKinsey aims to maintain:

(1) Technical competence.

(2) A reputation for superior management advice.

(3) Constant contact with businessmen.

One story illustrates the extent to which McKinsey people will go to carry out their focus. When efforts to contact a particular businessman through normal channels were unsuccessful, McKinsey rented an apartment next door to the person and used that base to make the businessman's acquaintance.

H.O. Hirt, founder of the Erie Insurance Group in Erie, Pennsylvania, expressed what he called "a simple business proposition" which has guided the company since its organization in 1925. Hirt said, "Sell the best possible protection at the lowest possible cost and back that up with the best possible service."

Erie Insurance, which conducts business in only eight states, does no advertising but is the nineteenth largest auto insurance company in America. Erie's growth in size and profitability has been based purely on word-of-mouth advertising — enthusiastic customers telling other people what a great job the company does.

Erie's philosophy was evident in 1986 when a disastrous tornado swept through northwestern Pennsylvania virtually wiping out the community of Albion.

The storm struck at 6:00 P.M. on a Friday. While other companies tried to figure out what to do, Erie went into action. They had adjusters on the scene on Saturday morning and had settled every total-loss claim by Sunday morning.

Rather than debating the depreciated value of their homes, Erie Insurance simply paid the homeowners the face value of their policies. Within one week, the company had settled all their claims in the community and was helping people get back on their feet.

It is this kind of service, based solely on Hirt's "business proposition," that has enabled the company to gain and sustain a competitive advantage in its market.

You Have to Keep the Legacy in Focus

We've just looked at several examples of a founder's values-oriented philosophy determining a company's focus. An adopted guiding light will grow dim and ineffective, however, if the beacon is not kept polished and in good repair as an organization develops and matures.

A continual reinforcement of the focus, the company mission or purpose, is necessary to maintain direction. Terrence Deal and Allen Kennedy looked into what makes companies with strong values-related philosophies so successful. They found that the companies had been able to develop a sort of family feeling or culture within their organization.[1] People who work for these companies consider themselves not merely employees, but a part of the company. Management does not retire to the eighth floor at 9:00 A.M. daily and come out and go for a drink with fellow executives at 5:00 P.M. They get to know their people. They talk about the mission and focus until everyone in the organization says "me too." From the housekeeping crew to the CEO, they're IBM people or GE people or DuPont people. Everybody buys into the mission. They identify with the "IBM Means Service" slogan or DuPont's "Better Things for Better Living through Chemistry," or GE's "We bring good things to life."

Books have been written and movies made about organizational cultures and the closeness that develops between fellow workers when they have a strong company focus. When the fictional workers gathered in the community bar for a beer after work, the foreman was present and was still the group leader.

Today we find this team spirit evident when management and employees of a small company show up to repaint office walls on a weekend day, to remodel an area, or to have a planning session; and when management, employees and family members of large organizations gather in their sports clothes on a Saturday to have a company picnic or to cheer for the company baseball team.

Executive Strategy Teams Can Sharpen Focus

One of the big questions we face in working with companies today is, "What do you do if you don't have the benefit of a charismatic founder?" In the absence of a philosophy from your founder, you create your own vision, your own focus. And the best way to accomplish that task is through an Executive Strategy Retreat.

Based on our work with top executive teams in a variety of organizations, from manufacturing to distribution, service businesses to health care and professional associations, we've been able to identify some techniques you can utilize to help establish a strong focus or philosophy:

(1) **Get key people on-board.** The first element in a successful Strategic Focus effort is to get the right people involved. We typically work closely with a top executive strategy team of ten to fifteen people, but we get input from everyone in the organization. The best people to serve on the strategic planning team are:

   (A) People who are in a position to have the vision to guide the organization, and

   (B) People in key roles who will be involved in the implementation of the strategy.

   In addition to those top-level people on the strategy team, it's important to get input from throughout the organization. Be sure your team specifically includes a representative from the following areas:

   • *The marketing department.* Key personnel should have significant input to offer and

will play prime roles in putting the Strategic Focus to work.

- *The sales force.* Members of the sales force
  are in daily contact with customers. If they
  are listening, they should have good information about customer expectations.
- *Customer service.* Getting input from
  customer service representatives and
  other customer problem solvers is important to determining focus and setting
  strategy.

(2) **Use both creative thinking and critical thinking.**
In our executive strategy retreats, we make a
special point to use creative thinking to generate
ideas and to separate creative thinking from
critical thinking. In creative thinking, we're
looking for large numbers of ideas and we don't
want those ideas to be inhibited by criticism,
comment or judgment. Therefore, we observe
the following guidelines in our creative-thinking
sessions:

   (A) *We suspend judgment.* We don't
       comment on any ideas. We simply get
       the idea before the group.

   (B) *We go for quantity, not quality.*
       Increative-thinking sessions, we try to
       generate as many ideas as possible with
       no concern for their quality.

   (C) *We make ideas visible.* In our strategy
       retreats, we use a technique called
       storyboarding. Other techniques for
       making ideas visible include flip charts,
       dry marker boards and chalkboards.

   (D) *We allow no speeches.* One of the best
       ways to stymie a creative-thinking
       session is to have some dominant
       person get up and give a speech.
       When contributing ideas in a

creative-thinking session, limit the
input to a few words and a maximum
of fifteen seconds of explanation.

(E) *We avoid killer phrases.* You've heard
them: "We've tried that before and it
didn't work." "That's not in the
budget." "We don't do it that way in
our company."

Once ideas have been created, they must be approached from
a critical mode. One of the failures of many of the brainstorming
sessions that are held in companies is that nothing is ever done
with the ideas that are generated.

How many times have you been in a session where somebody
gets a piece of chart paper, goes through a brainstorming session
and creates hundreds of good ideas, but nothing is done to
implement them. The goal is not to have 100 good ideas, but to
have three to five excellent ideas that you can put to work.

In our Executive Strategy Retreats, we use several methods
of critical thinking. After the group has created a list of ideas on
a specific topic, we review them several times to whittle the list
down to a workable size. We eliminate duplications. We look for
trends and recurring themes. We take out ideas that just don't
seem to fit or that can be effectively challenged by members of
the group.

Then it's time to prioritize the ideas. My preferred prioritizing criteria are impact and "doability." You can call them anything you wish.

By impact, I mean which ideas will have the greatest influ-
ence on the future success of the organization. Ideas with which
we can accomplish something are "doable." When you factor
those two criteria together, you can judge which ideas are most
likely to get implemented.

An important part of the critical thinking process is to attack
the ideas and not the people who suggested them. The storyboarding process helps keep criticism directed toward ideas.

Storyboarding Makes Ideas Visible

Storyboarding is a way to make ideas visible, a flexible way to organize and reorganize thoughts. It also serves as a way to get people involved and committed to a project. And it's a fun way to work hard. Basically, storyboarding involves using cork-boards, index cards, felt-tip markers and push pins to work with ideas.

Storyboarding is a technique that the Walt Disney organization brought into modern times, although the concept probably began with cave men who used wall paintings to tell stories. This communication method has been popular through the ages. Ancient Egyptians used hieroglyphics carved in stone to tell the stories of major events that occurred in their communities. Leonardo da Vinci was known to hang drawings of his inventions on the walls of his studio. I'm not sure what da Vinci used for push pins in that day, but his practice coincided with current storyboarding concepts.

Disney is most frequently credited with developing and promoting the use of storyboarding. He used it to create animated films and later in the planning and design of Disneyland and Walt Disney World.

I learned about storyboarding from former Disney employee, Mike Vance, and his student, Jerry McNellis. Vance taught creativity for Disney and was the dean of Disney University in Orlando. He now speaks and gives seminars on creativity. McNellis operates a creative planning center in New Brighton, Pennsylvania, and teaches facilitator training programs at Cuyahoga Community College near Cleveland, Ohio.

I have found storyboarding to be an extremely flexible and useful technique in almost any situation where I want to get input from a group of people. I use the technique in any type of client consultation, from Executive Strategy Retreats to market planning to the design of training programs and seminars or the development of customer satisfaction surveys.

Supplies for a storyboarding session are economical and easy to find. I use cork boards or bulletin boards. Two 3' by 4' sheets are ideal. I also use index cards in several sizes (5" X 7", 4" X 6", 3" X 5") and in several colors, push pins and wide felt markers.

First, Clarify Your Objective

Start your storyboarding session by defining the problem, concern or opportunity you will deal with. Outline what you want to accomplish, then focus on your specific objectives. Once you know what your goals are, you can get right down to brainstorming and producing ideas.

The session facilitator is responsible for getting the ideas to develop. One way to do that is to identify a series of headers or categories which will stimulate participant thinking.

Let's use stakeholder expectations as an example of a typical storyboarding session.

I, as facilitator, begin the process by asking participants to identify organization stakeholders. Stakeholders, you will remember, are defined as groups of individuals who have some stake in the success or failure of an organization.

The group might identify twenty or thirty different individuals or groups of people who have a stake in their organization. They write down each suggestion on a separate index card, and I pin the cards on the storyboard. We then prioritize that list using stick-on red dots. By sticking the dots on the cards, participants can vote for the stakeholders they think are most important to the company. It is easy, at that point, to arrange the suggested stakeholders in order of presumed importance. Whoever has the most red dots wins.

I can easily pick the top seven stakeholder groups, arrange those cards across the top of the board, and then ask the strategy team to list the expectations of each group.

Typical stakeholder headings might be customers, employees, shareholders, supplier, and the community.

Considering each of the headings, we ask ourselves, "What does this group expect from our company or organization?" Ideas are tossed out non-judgmentally. Again, we create a long list of possible expectations, sort out the duplicates, throw away the ones we agree do not fit and prioritize the remaining list using the red dot method. When you finish the exercise, you may have several boards full of prioritized lists of stakeholder expectations. This is a treasure trove for action.

We use the same technique to identify strengths, weaknesses, opportunities or threats. Storyboarding can also be used to help a group write a statement of mission or purpose or to identify strategy actions or goals.

I use storyboarding to develop marketing plans and to design training programs. It's particularly effective in developing a customized training program to support implementation of an organization's corporate strategy or Strategic Focus.

Sharpen Focus by Segmenting Your Market

Another technique that is helpful in sharpening the focus of an organization is to take markets or groups of customers or stakeholders and break them down into small segments. I use the "market cube" theory.

Imagine, if you will, a three-dimensional cube similar to the Rubic's Cube in which each dimension is divided into sub-categories. We may divide the bottom dimension into customer types; the vertical dimension can include product or service categories; the depth dimension can stand for geographic markets.

By breaking down your customers, your products, and your geographic markets, you divide the large cube into many smaller cubes — each a market segment.

Once you've developed an understanding of the various segments of your market, you will need to conduct a market-gap analysis. A market-gap analysis involves considering each market segment in order to uncover unmet customer needs. I break the analysis process down into the following steps:

(A) *Establish criteria for desirable markets, and separate the criteria into "musts" and "wants."* A must is a criteria that absolutely has to be met for an area to be an acceptable market segment. Wants are highly desirable features.

(B) *Dissect the market cube.* Separate each of the small market segments.

(C) *Identify potential opportunities from your customers' "worry list."* That is, look at each of the market segments and get a clear picture of the customers that make up that segment. Do some creative thinking, or better yet, talk to the customers. Learn about the key items on their list of concerns. What are their chief sources of frustration or anxiety?

(D) *Identify products and services to address the customer's worries.* In this step you look at the capabilities of your firm and at the concerns of customers in each market segment and try to identify opportunities where you can match your products and services to the customer's needs and wants.

(E) *Eliminate opportunities which don't meet the criteria.*
At this point, you match the potential target
market segments with the criteria that you
established in Step A, and eliminate those
opportunities that don't fit. You can use this
method of critical thinking to break down a long
list of opportunities into a more manageable list.

(F) *Prioritize your lists of opportunities.* In your
prioritizing, you might use again the "impact"
and "doability" criteria. Look at the potential
target markets. In which markets would you
have the greatest opportunities for impact in
terms of products and services? Are there
markets you are unable to address? You need to
be able to clearly define the market and identify
potential customers within that category. You
may be able to match a particular ability or
unique product that you have with a particular
market segment. When you look closely at
available opportunities, you may locate a
potential market segment that offers a very
narrow market niche and few competitors.

(G) *Verify your opportunities.* Go out and talk to
customers in your targeted market segment.
Talk to other vendors competing in that market
to verify that your assumptions or ideas are valid.

(H) *Do a competitive analysis.* In this step, you identify
all firms who provide competing products or
services or who may be competing with you for
revenue dollars. In some instances, your
competitors will be offering products and
services that perform the same function as yours
do. In other instances, you may be competing
with products or services dissimilar to yours, but
ones which might consume revenue dollars that
would otherwise be spent with your company.

Wally Barnes, Chairman of the Board of the Bristol, Connecticut, based Barnes Group, had this to say a year after their first Executive Strategy Retreat:

> We're competing better in the various markets we serve already. We have become more focused, more selective about the markets we want to serve. One of the great weaknesses of our company in the past is that we were really trying to be all things to all people. We now realize that it isn't possible, nor is it advisable. We are operating much more efficiently in the markets we choose to serve, because we are concentrating on those individual markets and are not distracted by some of the periferal markets.

Dick Hines, former group vice president for Associated Spring, an operating unit of The Barnes Group, gave us a specific example of what Wally was talking about. Dick has a division in Gardena, California, which once manufactured five different lines of springs. Three different Associated Spring plants made one of those products, brake springs for trucks. The people at Gardena decided to focus. They selected truck brake springs as their target market.

Today, Associated Spring owns eighty percent of the truck brake spring business in the United States, and there is only one small competitor. "This example goes to show you," says Dick, "that if you focus, you can really improve your market share "

Effective Strategic Focus Requires Consensus

An important step in developing an effective Strategic Focus is for members of the organizational strategy team to reach a consensus. I believe a high level of ownership of and commitment to a focus will develop only when all members of a team agree on the plan. One of the greatest factors contributing to failure of organizations to implement their strategy is lack of commitment or ownership in the plan by key executives. This void is more apt to occur when the strategy is developed by only one person, or a small group of people, without input or consideration from others who will be responsible for implementing the strategy.

I have found that the most effective way to have the whole team buy into a Strategic Focus is through participation in an Executive Strategy Retreat. The retreat is a two-and-one-half or three-day, off-site planning session using an experienced facilitator and the storyboarding process to get the input of all members of the strategy team and, through them, the input of their key managers and support people.

Chapter seven will describe in detail how to hold an Executive Strategy Retreat.

KEY POINTS

(1) Strategic Focus does not come automatically; nor is it permanent. It must be pursued vigorously until it is razor sharp, then resharpened constantly.

(2) There are two ways to arrive at Strategic Focus:

    (A) Some organizations inherit a guiding purpose from their founder.

    (B) Some organizations create an effective focus through careful analysis of their reason for existence.

(3) To be an effective beacon, company focus must be kept in focus.

(4) Cultivating a company culture helps reinforce focus.

(5) To have an effective strategic planning team, you have to have the right people on board.

(6) Effective strategic thinking requires both creative and critical thinking.

(7) The key is not to have 100 good ideas, but to have three to five excellent ideas that you can put to work.

(8) Storyboarding is a flexible system to use in creating ideas and reaching conclusions.

(9) Effective Strategic Focus requires consensus.

NOTES:

[1] Terrence E. Deal and Allen A. Kennedy, *Corporate Cultures* (Reading, MA: Addison-Wesley Publishing Company, 1982), p. 7-12.

CHAPTER SEVEN

Staging A Successful Executive Strategy Retreat

PURPOSE: *To give specific information about conducting Executive Strategy Retreats as we do them in our consulting practice to help clients set strategy.*

Strategic Focus frequently gets pushed aside by "urgent" matters (many of which grow out of a lack of Strategic Focus) in the day-to-day running of a business. The only way to give Strategic Focus the attention it deserves is to block out enough time and make it priority one for all key people. In other words, hold an Executive Strategy Retreat, which we refer to as an ESR.

What is an ESR? It's 2-1/2 days away from headquarters. It's no telephone calls, no interruptions. It's an organization's leaders meeting to focus their undivided attention on key issues facing the organization. And, it's an excellent team-building experience.

Getting top-level executives away from day-to-day decisions, problems and interruptions is important in setting the stage for strategic thinking. Many organizations use get-away meetings, but few of them manage those meetings effectively, and often

97

such an event provides little more than an excuse to get away and play golf.

Any time I start to help an organization plan an ESR, I'm reminded of this anonymous piece. And, although it's good for a laugh, the situation it describes is one a good facilitator will seek to avoid.

> In the beginning, God created the heavens and the earth. The earth was without form and void; so God created a small committee. God carefully balanced the committee as to sex, ethnic origin and economic status in order to interface pluralism with the holistic concept of self-determinism according to judicatory guidelines. Even God was impressed. And so ended the first day.

> And God said, "Let the committee draw up a mission statement." And behold, the committee decided to prioritize and strategize. And God called the process "empowerment." And God thought it sounded pretty good. And there was evening and there was morning, the second day.

> And God said, "Let the committee determine goals and objectives and engage in long-range planning." Unfortunately a debate as to the semantic difference between the goals and objectives pre-empted almost all of the third day. Although the question was never satisfactorily resolved, God thought the process was constructive. And there was evening and there was morning, the third day.

> And God said, "Let there be a retreat in which the committee can envision functional organization and engage in planning by objectives." The committee considered adjustment of priorities and consequent alternatives to program direction. And God saw that this was good. And God thought it was even worth all the coffee and doughnuts he had to supply. And so ended the fourth day.

> And God said, "Let the program be implemented consistent with long-range planning and strategy." The com-

mittee considered guidelines, linkages, structural sensitivities, alternatives and implementational models. And God saw that this was very democratic. And so would have ended the fifth day except for the unintentional renewal of the debate about the differences between goals and objectives.

On the sixth day the committee agreed on criteria for judicatory assessment and evaluation. This wasn't the agenda God had planned. He wasn't able to attend the meeting, however, because He had to take the afternoon off to create day and night and heaven and earth, and seas and plants and trees, and seasons and years, and sun and moon, and birds and fish and animals and human beings.

On the seventh day God rested and the committee submitted its recommendations. It turned out that the recommended form for things was nearly identical to the way God had already created them, so the committee passed a resolution commending God for His implementation according to guidelines. There was, however, some opinion expressed quietly that human beings should have been created in the committee's image.

And God caused a deep sleep to fall on the committee...

Anonymous

Seriously, there are a lot of factors to be considered when planning an ESR. Conducting a productive event requires attention to such matters as who will participate, where the retreat will be held, what items will be included on the agenda and who will serve as facilitator.

How to Select the Strategy Team

An important early step in planning an effective retreat is determining who should participate. I have found that the ideal group size is eleven to fifteen people. Actually, in terms of creative thinking and problem solving, a group of five to seven people is probably more productive. In working with a variety of organizations, our firm has found that we could not keep participant level that low. We have also learned that when we have gotten above eighteen to twenty people, the group is unwieldy.

Working with eleven to fifteen people has been a satisfactory compromise. That is enough people to remain involved and committed to the process, but not so many that the process becomes unmanageable.

There are two primary criteria for selecting members of the retreat team:

(1) Select members of top management who have the vision to set direction for the company. It is their understanding of the organization and their perception of the marketplace which gives them the ability to create the vision.

(2) Include people who will be in positions to implement the strategy that the team will develop.

The chief executive officer will make the ultimate decision on who will attend the strategy retreat. It isn't an easy decision. In a large company, participants will probably be selected from across layers of management. Typically, a CEO will have only three to five people reporting directly to him or her, but the next level may include twenty to twenty-five executives. Of course, all the enthusiastic, ambitious executives want to be included in a session to determine corporate philosophy or direction.

To limit participants to fifteen, the CEO must decide who to invite and who to exclude on that second level. Often we find that at the second management level there are representatives from sales, marketing, human resources, management information systems and other key staff groups who will be involved in implementing the strategic plan.

The CEO must give consideration to communicating with persons who are not included in the retreat. Without their support and commitment, the Strategic Focus will flounder. It's important to make it clear up front that although every important member of the management team cannot participate in the retreat, their input and support will be solicited, indeed required, in order for the event to be effective.

What Features Make For a Good Retreat Site?

We've conducted retreats in a wide variety of settings -- some sites we found conducive to a productive meeting and some actually interfered with getting our job done. With that experience in mind, let me suggest some guidelines for Executive Strategy Retreat site selection:

(1) Select a facility fifty to seventy-five miles away from your office. The site should have:

    (A) Comfortable lodging

    (B) A well-lit, well-ventilated meeting room

    (C) Some form of recreation available (swimming pool or tennis court)

    (D) A hospitality suite

    (E) Good food and timely service

(2) Find a facility that will provide a single contact person with whom you can work. That contact should agree to be on the site throughout the working day.

(3) Avoid booking a large convention facility. Most convention centers are set up to handle groups of several hundred to several thousand. A group of fifteen will get lost in the shuffle.

(4) Do not select a hotel that caters to golf, skiing or some other major recreational activity. Individuals on the site for such activity will be noisy and distracting and the facility will tend to cater to the golfers or the skiers, rather than to a group of executives who have come to meet and work.

When choosing your strategy retreat site, keep in mind that it is not necessary to go a long distance from the home office, but it is important to be far enough away to minimize interruptions from telephones.

What Goes on the Agenda?

Here is a sample agenda that we use with many of our clients. This particular agenda is adjustable to suit individual organizational needs, but offers a number of features that I have found very effective for accomplishing the purpose of an Executive Strategy Retreat.

Typically the retreat begins in late afternoon with check-in, followed by a brief cocktail hour or social time and dinner.

Immediately after dinner we hold an introductory work session which lasts until about 9:30 P.M.

The next morning we get an early breakfast and start a work session by eight o'clock, work through noon, break for one hour and come back to work from 1:00 P.M. to 4:00 P.M. Following a couple of hours for rest and recreation, we meet for dinner, followed by another work session.

The third day follows much the same pattern except we try to finish up by about 3:00 P.M.

Some facilitators would argue against cocktails and against evening sessions. I have found, however, that both those events contribute to the process. The opening cocktail hour or social hour is a good ice breaker and allows the strategy team to get comfortable with one another in an informal setting. Many top executives only interact with others in their company formally in meetings, and dressed in their blue suits and white shirts. Sitting around the hospitality suite in a sport shirt with a glass of wine and some cheese is a new experience. The informality of this social time sets the stage for the rest of the retreat.

The first evening session serves to introduce the format and prepare participants for the intense sessions which start early the following morning.

I usually open the first strategy retreat session with a brief description of the Model of Strategic Thinking which we will use later in the session, and an introduction to the storyboarding process. Then we warm up by using the storyboard to define the

AGENDA

Wednesday

5:30 to 6:00 P.M.	Arrival, Check-in, Social Time
6:00 to 7:00	Dinner
7:00 to 10:00	Work Session
	Introduction to Strategic Thinking
	Stakeholder Expectations

Thursday

7:00 to 8:00	Breakfast
8:00 to 12:00	Work Session
	Five Types of Vision
	Mission
	Values
12:00 to 1:00	Lunch
1:00 to 4:00	Work Session
	Complete Guiding Philosophy
	Critical Measures of Success
	Unique Factor
4:00 to 6:00	Recreation
6:00 to 7:30	Dinner
7:30 to 9:00	Work Session
	Target Markets

Friday

7:00 to 8:00	Breakfast
8:00 to 12:00	Work Session
	S.W.O.T. Analysis
	Basic Assumptions
12:00 to 1:00	Lunch
1:00 to 3:00	Work Session
	Strategic Actions
	Strategy Communication
	Plan for Continued Action
3:00	Adjourn

elements of the organization's mission and purpose and to discuss the business we're in.

Then We Really Get Down to Business

Day two is a long one running from 8:00 A.M. to 9:30 or 10:00 in the evening. It's an intensive day, but a day when the group really gets cooking, and generally the participants want to work as long as they can.

I usually schedule a break from 4:00 P.M. to 6:00 P.M. for rest and recreation. Some groups will play a little tennis, swim, take a walk or a nap. Occasionally a group will try to squeeze in nine holes of golf.

A number of my clients have asked to adjust the schedule and to quit a little earlier so they can play eighteen holes of golf, but I don't recommend that on the first retreat.

On several occasions recently, I have agreed to that schedule, only to find that we never did get to the golf course. By the time the group returns from lunch and gets back into storyboarding their strategy, they are so intent on the process and the outcome that they don't want to quit. They invariably cancel their tee times. The fact that they have tee times scheduled and cannot get there is a source of frustration and interrupts the flow of our work.

I suggest that, at least during the first retreat, recreation be kept to the site and within the two-hour allotted break. Follow-up sessions or subsequent retreats may allow for more recreation time.

An important part of the process is keeping on schedule. Start when you say you will start and end when you say you will end. Predicting exactly what you will be discussing during each work session is difficult, but you should have a pretty clear outline of the topics to be discussed during the event and you should keep to your agenda.

The Facilitator Keeps the Retreat on Track

I am absolutely convinced that a facilitator from outside an organization enhances the effectiveness of an ESR. As an objective outsider, a facilitator's role includes:

(1) Establishing the agenda
(2) Facilitating the storyboarding process
(3) Keeping the group focused on its task
(4) Enforcing the rules of creative thinking
(5) Leading the critical thinking process
(6) Insuring equal participation
(7) Providing personal guidance to the CEO

An Executive Strategy Retreat is one of the few opportunities for several layers of management to work together freely. The retreat offers an open forum for'input of fresh ideas and new thinking a forum through which lower-level management can make contributions to an organization's direction. Top-level managers who've been isolated in their executive suites a long time usually appreciate the opportunity to work with energetic young executives in the company.

An important aspect of reaching an acceptable consensus is to be sure that everybody in the group approaches the task as equals. We sit around a U-shaped table with the open side of the U facing the storyboards. As the facilitator, I lead the discussion, collect the cards, pin the cards on the boards, enforce the rules and make sure no one dominates a session.

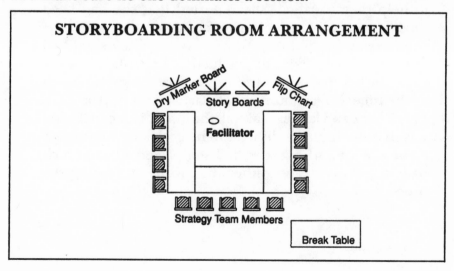

STORYBOARDING ROOM ARRANGEMENT

Dry Marker Board   Story Boards   Flip Chart

Facilitator

Strategy Team Members

Break Table

I typically clarify my facilitating role with the CEO before the retreat to be sure that we are in agreement that this will be a participative process and that our objective is to reach consensus of the group, not to simply reflect the CEO's thinking.

As facilitator, I come to the group to direct the retreat process. I focus my energies on understanding the process, communicating the process and leading the event, but I make no contributions to content. I do tell stories and use anecdotes to stimulate thinking, but do not get involved in guiding the content discussed. That's the role of the participants.

A recent experience reinforced my thinking on the importance of using an outside facilitator in conducting a productive strategy retreat.

A client, who is the director of a health-care group, is also president of the state professional organization. She asked me to facilitate the strategic thinking process with the board of the association.

I was able to spend two full days with the group and we got a lot done, but they decided that they needed another day. I was unavailable on the day they chose, so I helped the president prepare an agenda and gave her some coaching on the use of storyboarding.

At the end of the day, she called to ask if I would return to help them further. She reported that she had been unable to remain an objective facilitator; that when she tried to stay out of the input process, the discussions had tended to take off on unproductive tangents; and that since she was president and was before the group much of the time as facilitator, other participants appeared to just sit back and let her make all the input. Her conclusion was that she found it difficult to be both a facilitator and a participant and had decided she preferred to participate in the discussion rather than focus on leading the process.

There Shall Be No Quiet Observers

There is no space around the table at a strategy planning session for a quiet observer. It's an enthusiastic, involving process. Storyboarding supports that idea. Storyboarding allows for a high energy level and encourages participation by everyone in the room.

When a group is in a creative-thinking mode and the ideas are flowing, you can fill a 3' X 4' storyboard with 3" X 5" index cards in just a few minutes. We encourage full participation by clearly establishing a "no-critique, no-comments" ground rule for storyboarding sessions. Participants will be enthusiastic and produce fresh ideas when they know there will be no criticism or feedback about their ideas at the creative stage.

And finally, you must maintain an atmosphere of equal participation throughout the event. A CEO who dominates an Executive Strategy Retreat might as well keep his people at home and on the job waiting for edicts from above to tell them which direction the company will go and what moves they should make. Setting fifteen company people up to a weekend out of town can be expensive, particularly if the CEO is merely going to reiterate his or her thinking.

In all the retreats that I have lead, I have only had one instance in which the CEO thoroughly dominated the discussion. And that was at a follow-up planning session rather than at the initial retreat.

We had spent 2-1/2 days conducting the retreat and needed some additional work. A day-long session was scheduled in the same city as the client organization. We set the planning day at a private social club in the downtown area and arrived to find that the club's meeting room had a long, narrow conference table rather than the preferred U-shaped setup we were accustomed to using.

Unfortunately, the seating arrangement ended with me at one end of the table and the president at the other. As we tried to storyboard some ideas, we found that the dialog went from me to the president and back. I asked the questions and he answered them. There was very little participation from other team members.

After several unproductive hours, I stopped the process and conducted what is called a "yama." I asked several different people in the group at random, "How do you feel right now?" Their responses were pretty clear. They thought the process was not working.

I suggested that we stop for the day, go back to the office and continue regular work there, and reconvene the strategy session later. This gave me a chance to meet with the training manager and the president to assess what had gone wrong and to develop ideas to prevent its happening again. It was a learning experience.

We identified a few problems, among them: We were all in our blue suits, we were at a long narrow conference table and we were too close to the office. The session had taken on the aura of other meetings in the organization. We corrected the situation by insisting on a U-shaped table, by gathering in a more casual setting, and by using the storyboarding process more effectively to minimize the opportunity for one person to dominate the input.

It Isn't Over When It's Over
Document Your Results

An important part of an Executive Strategy Retreat is to accurately document the discussion that took place. Storyboarding can also make the documenting task easier. I take two strips of 1/2" masking tape and run them down the face of the cards -- right over the printing -- then pull the pins, fold up the strips of cards, slip them into an envelope and take them back to the office.

We enter the data into a computer and print out a summary of the event for each member of the strategy team. It's a quick, easy way to document the meeting for participants, and it gives them material to refer to as the thinking and planning process continues between the initial retreat and follow-up sessions. I have shortened the reporting-time process by taking a micro-cassette tape recorder with me and dictating the information from the cards before I leave the retreat site. This allows my office staff to transcribe the tape and create the document more quickly. I save the cards as back-up to check for content.

And Then...We Meet Again

My experience is that to get through the entire strategic-thinking process in just 2-1/2 days is impossible. Consequently, follow-up sessions are a necessity. In typical situations, I recommend monthly full-day sessions for three to six months after the initial retreat. In lieu of the day sessions, some groups prefer to have a second 2-1/2-day retreat about six weeks after the first one.

We continue using the strategic-thinking process and plugging details into the plan during those sessions. And we create a report a session document for each team member following each meeting.

After all the follow-up sessions are complete and we have gone through the entire strategic-thinking process, my staff and I go back and revise the entire document and create a Strategy Book.

The STRATEGY BOOK

The Strategy Book looks common enough, but it contains the plan that can make the difference in an organization's competitive position in the marketplace.

The Strategy Book is a 1-1/2", three-ring binder with a series of tabs. The book ends up having twenty-five to thirty typewritten pages and becomes a working document that members of the strategy team will use to guide decision making and to monitor implementation.

The book, which will be discussed in more detail in the next chapter, includes the following divisions:

(A) *Strategic profile* — a picture of the organization and its position in the marketplace.

(B) *Values statements* — mission and other such values statements as the guiding philosophy, unique factor and driving force.

(C) *Strategy statement* — a summary of the Strategic Focus and actions the organization must take to carry out the focus.

(D) *Communication plan* — describes how the strategy team will communicate the Strategic Focus to the rest of the organization.

(E) *Strategic actions* — lists, with a separate tab, each activity which will be used to accomplished the strategic action.

KEY POINTS

(1) Executive Strategy Retreats provide opportunity for a team of top-level executives to concentrate on developing an organizational strategy plan.

(2) The retreat site should provide an environment conducive to uninterrupted work.

(3) The agenda is planned to create an effective schedule of work and recreation.

(4) An effective retreat depends on a highly skilled, objective facilitator from outside the organization.

(5) The storyboarding system encourages group-wide input and provides a format that allows for rapid creation and organization of ideas.

(6) An accurate document of retreat activity is vital to strategy implementation.

(7) Follow-up meetings are usually required to wrap up the strategic thinking and planning process.

(8) A Strategy Book provides a record of an organization's strategic thinking and plan for action.

CHAPTER EIGHT

How to Use a Model of Strategic Thinking

PURPOSE: *To explain the Tweed model of strategic thinking and to demonstrate how it is used to stimulate discussion and guide the strategy-setting process.*

Why is it necessary to have a strategic thinking model? It's your blueprint for action. I have found over the years that to facilitate the strategic-thinking process, having a plan is important. Just like you must have a plan for your business, you must have a plan for the strategy-setting process.

It's particularly helpful to approach the Executive Strategy Retreat with a model for strategic thinking. A model is a visual display of the process that will be used. Below is a graphic depiction of the model I use when guiding an organization's strategic development.

The model I use has three major components: a strategic profile, a section on vision and values, and a strategy statement. The first segment begins with where we are now as an organization, the third segment looks at where we want to be in the future, and the middle segment describes the mission and values that will help guide our actions and decisions as we move from where

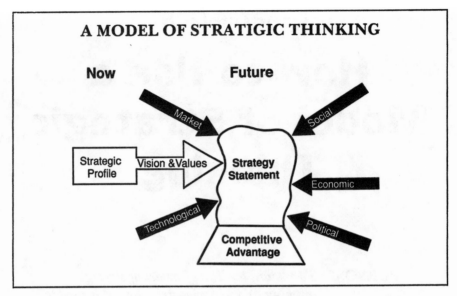

we are to where we want to be. Let's look in more depth at each component.

The Strategic Profile

The strategic profile describes the organization as it is today. It includes stakeholder expectations, a current mission statement, a description of the markets served, customer profiles, a competitive analysis, buying motives, success factors, and a prioritized list of company strengths, weaknesses, opportunities and threats. We usually include a strategy-team opinionnaire, a one-page financial summary, and a brief market summary including competitor analysis in the profile section.

The first section is a quick snapshot. It is not a detailed analysis of huge amounts of data. Some people might argue that it is necessary to have a lot of data before beginning the strategic-thinking process. Let me share some past consulting experiences that support my theory.

I have been called by at least a dozen organizations to help with strategic thinking after these companies had already attempted to develop a plan. Here's what I found.

Typically, the organization will have spent many expensive hours with a consulting firm conducting analysis and gathering data. The data will have been summarized in a three-inch, three-ring binder that is overwhelming. The consulting firm will usually also have met with members of the top executive team and formulated a strategy based partly on input from the team and partly on experience of the consultants.

The result of this latter process is a written strategic plan that fills up another three-inch, three-ring binder with background, mission, goals, objectives, action steps and recommendations. It, too, is overwhelming.

Everybody looks at the intimidating notebooks and puts off reading them until "next week." The problems that initiated the strategizing activity in the first place multiply and the organization turns for help to another consultant.

I go into the organization and find the previous strategic plan collecting dust on the CEO's book shelf. On several occasions, when we have completed the strategic thinking process and I compare their old plan to our new one, I find many similarities between the two. The primary difference between the old document and ours is in the strategy team's commitment to and ownership of the plan. So, rather than go into an extensive data collection and analysis process, I have found the "quick snapshot" system more productive.

During the ESR, we add to the items we have collected the team's perception of strengths, weaknesses, opportunities and threats (SWOT), and stakeholder expectations. The SWOT and stakeholder information is based on the team's knowledge of and experience in the business.

Let me note here that I find that if the top-executive team does not have a good gut feel for the business, we're wasting our efforts bringing them together in a strategy retreat. You can amass all the data you want, do all the analyses you want and draw up all the strategy you want, but if an organization's top executives don't know their business, neither the strategic-planning process nor the executives will be successful.

The Values Section

The values section of our model contains the basic beliefs or values which guide the organization's decision making. This is the real heart of strategy formulation. Organizations that have clear values tend to be more successful than those that do not. Values include the organization's driving force, the unique factor and the guiding philosophy. Some strategy teams also discuss how they want to position the company in the mind of the customer.

Successful individuals and successful organizations tend to have a focus, or a single focal point. Maybe it's a clear purpose. Maybe it's a clear focus on how they can best serve their customers. Whichever, these clearly focused organizations know who they are, who their customers are and what their customers expect from them.

We talked in earlier chapters about the importance to an organization of a clear purpose and philosophies or values to guide day-to-day decision making. As the head of a small catering firm said, "What I want is a statement that will guide the thinking of our people on a day-to-day basis. When a crew is at a party and it's 9:00 P.M. and the bread tray is getting low and they're debating whether to put out some rolls left from yesterday's affair or return to the central kitchen for freshly baked bread, I want those employees to have some basis for making that judgment."

Every organization has a 9:00 P.M.-empty-bread-tray situation where people need to make a decision. You're trusting the fate of your company to those people, so it's important that they understand the philosophy of the business.

In developing this section of our strategic thinking model, we work through the process of creating that mission and values.

Another important discussion which we include in the values section of an ESR is a determination or definition of the organization's unique factor. The unique factor is a "Walt Disneyism." The unique factor is what differentiates your firm or your products from those of your competition. Disney used to say that if you want to be successful in business, you must make yourself unique by being so good at what you do that people have to come to you to get what you have.

The unique factor is both the basis for Strategic Focus and the basis for competitive advantage. In an earlier chapter we discussed five sources of competitive advantage. The way in which your firm creates its combination of those competitive advantage factors makes you unique.

An organization's driving force is another area which we address in the values-clarification period of a strategy retreat. The driving force concept was developed by Ben Tregoe and John Zimmerman of the Kepner-Tregoe organization in Princeton, New Jersey, and described in their book *Top Management Strategy*.[1]

Tregoe and Zimmerman maintain that the driving force is the strategic area which is most important in determining a company's future products and markets. The authors suggest that if a company can select one factor as their driving force, they will be able to make consistent decisions when it comes time to decide about a new product or a new market. I have found that conducting the driving-force discussion early in a retreat has a positive, gelling affect on the direction of the event. It gets all members of the team thinking in the same direction, heading for the same flag on the green, and results in a strong organization.

Creative Pultrusions, a small manufacturer of fiberglass components for the transportation, chemical and electrical utility industries, uses ESRs to effectively set their sights and define their direction.

Even though the organization is small — about seventy-five employees, twenty of whom are managers, supervisors and engineers — it was firmly established and withstood a difficult economic downturn in the early '80s. When the economy faltered, Creative Pultrusions already had a five-year plan in place and were conducting ESRs every six months to review their position and continue education and team-building activities.

Creative Pultrusions was able to stick to their strategy and their values. They were persistent in maintaining their Strategic Focus. Today, they are the second largest pultruder in the country, and very profitable.

According to Bob Sweet, founder and president of the company, "The strategic thinking process we began using nearly ten years ago has helped us in our day-to-day decision making. Our business has grown, our people have grown and our problems

have grown, but our values have stayed the same. The result is
many long term successful relationships with key customers, and
with our employees."

The Strategy Statement

The strategy statement consists of strategic objectives, a "superordinate goal," strategic actions that must be taken to achieve
the company's mission, and a strategy summary. It is a one-page
summary of the Strategic Focus and capabilities which must be
developed in order to implement the focus. It also includes a
summary of planned strategic actions.

The strategy statement is supported by basic assumptions
about what an organization's leaders believe will happen in the
future.

The shape of the strategy statement is molded by the following external influences:

(1) Market forces
(2) Technological forces
(3) Social forces
(4) Economic forces
(5) Political forces

The uncertainty of these forces causes the shape of the
strategy statement to be irregular. Unlike the strategic profile,
which is a nice, neat rectangle because the profile is clearly
defined.

The strategy statement is uneven and irregular because we
don't have a way of knowing what the ongoing impact of these
outside forces will be. The uncertainty we face in the business
environment today makes it impossible for us to plan in great
detail beyond one or two years.

Since we cannot predict the future, the chief purpose of an
ESR is to prepare an organization to effectively operate in the
business climate, however it may evolve.

The astute Executive Strategy Team must spend time discussing and reaching conclusions on each of these issues in
formulating Strategic Focus for the organization. Anticipating
the outside forces affecting a company and making some state-

ments about what the leadership believes will happen becomes the base upon which they build strategy.

Obviously the assumptions on which an organization bases its strategy must be continually verified through data gathering and monitoring of the environment.

Strategic Actions Follow Strategic Thinking

Strategic actions that evolve during an ESR are statements describing broad activity which the organization expects to undertake to gain and sustain their competitive edge in the marketplace.

Varying from company to company, the planned strategic actions usually involve development of systems to achieve an organization's strategy and the development of employees to carry through on those systems. This combination and coordination of systems and trained people enables a corporation to be competitive to successfully implement its overall strategy. There are also strategic actions to measure perceptions, such as customer perception and employee perception.

Usually, we find that organizations have three to five strategic actions that affect the whole company. And each functional area may have one or two strategic actions that are specific to their area but affect the overall strategy.

And, of course, the implementation of strategy determines the success of the ESR system of thinking and planning and the ultimate success of the organization. We will discuss implementation in more detail in Chapter Ten, "The Strategy Diamond ™."

KEY POINTS

(1) A strategic thinking model is a blueprint for action.

(2) The Tweed strategic thinking model has three major components: a strategic profile, a section on mission and values, and a strategy statement.

   (A) The strategic profile describes the organization as it is today.

   (B) The values section contains the basic

beliefs which guide the organization's decision making.

(C) The strategy statement consists of objectives, a "superordinate goal," actions that must be taken to achieve the company's mission, and a strategy summary.

(3) The strategy statement is influenced by the impact of outside forces on an organization.

(4) Strategic actions that evolve during an ESR are statements describing broad activity which the organization expects to undertake to gain and sustain a competitive edge in the marketplace.

(5) A combination and coordination of systems and trained people will enable a corporation to successfully implement its overall strategy.

(6) The implementation of an organization's strategy will determine the success of the ESR system of thinking and planning and the ultimate success of an organization.

NOTES:

[1]Ben Tregoe and John Zimmerman, *Top Management Strategy* (New York: Simon and Schuster, 1980).

CHAPTER NINE

How to Make Every Person in Your Organization Understand and Care About Your Focus

PURPOSE: *To give specific techniques that can be used to communicate the Strategic Focus, mission and values to every person within the organization.*

If Strategic Focus is to produce long-term, measurable results, every person within an organization must understand it and be committed to making it happen. The Strategic Focus can only come alive when it is *effectively* communicated.

Although communicating the Strategic Focus is not a one-time event, but an on-going process, the initial presentation of the strategy should be well planned and carried out with a certain amount of pizazz and hoopla. My experience with a variety of organizations suggests that the more enthusiasm and fun associated with introducing the Strategic Focus the more likely it is to catch fire among employees.

When you can spotlight long-term objectives and get everybody in an organization Identifying with them, there is virtually no limit to what you can do. That process, of course, requires frequent reviewing of the mission statement or a catch phrase or motto — something you can use to bind members of the organization together.

Let's look at the two chief divisions in Strategic Focus communication: the initial introduction of the ideas and plan and the ongoing reinforcement of corporate strategy. First, we will consider factors involved in planning organization-wide introduction of the Strategic Focus.

What Do You Tell Whom?

When you are planning your initial corporate communication strategy, the first considerations are:

(1) What sections of the strategic plan do we communicate to which levels of the organization?

(2) What is privileged information? What must be guarded and why? What types of decisions or information must be restricted and communicated at the proper time?

(3) What methods should we use to communicate the strategy throughout the organization?

In deciding what to tell to whom, I often draw a matrix on a dry-marker board and have the strategy team discuss what information should be communicated to which group.

Across the top of the matrix are the various levels of the organization. For example, I would include board of directors, executive strategy team, department heads, managers, supervisors, and other employees.

Down the vertical scale of the matrix are the various elements of the strategy: mission, guiding philosophy, values, strategy statement, strategic actions, operating plan, department plans.

Although the elements will vary from one organization to another, a visual display of the communication will usually look like this:

EXECUTIVE STRATEGY COMMUNICATION PLAN

	Board of Directors	Executive Team	Dept. Heads Group Mgrs.	Managers Branch Mgrs	Supervisors	Employees
Mission						
Guiding Philosophy						
Values						
Strategy Statement						
Strategic Actions				(Revised version written for distribution)		
Strategic Goals						
Operating Plan						
Department Plans						

= = Printed copies provided. Information will be communicated to all in this group.

As part of the discussion on the communication plan, we determine what information to control. The management of many companies have the mistaken perception that much strategic information should not be made public. My experience with a variety of organizations suggests that there are only three types of information which cannot and should not be disclosed:

(1) Confidential personnel actions. No information related to the employment of a particular individual should be released.

(2) Information on mergers and acquisitions. Generally this information must be controlled because the other party in the merger or acquisition requests confidentiality. In publicly traded companies there are some Securities and Exchange Commission rules and regulations that prohibit executives from disclosing information about potential mergers or acquisitions or from using that information to trade in either company's stock.

(3) Information relating to pending patents or other
     contract negotiations such as branch openings or
     closings where disclosure could result in a
     competitor taking action that would have adverse
     consequences on your company

Any other information about plans, policies, procedures or
performance should be openly communicated by managers and
supervisors. The sharing of information serves to cement employee "ownership" of the organization's mission and strategy.

In dealing with chief executives in several highly successful
organizations, I have found that they are more than willing to
share openly any information about their company outside of
the above categories.

Employees better identify with their company when they
know the boss. CEO's need to be seen and heard to give their
company an identity. Whether the message going out is good or
bad, the CEO should deliver it, directly.

Chet Giermak, president of Eriez Magnetics, has regular
meetings with all employees to disclose financial information,
company performance and any news that may be of interest to
the employees. Even though Eriez is a privately held, family-
owned business, they have no hesitation about disclosing specific
financial results. Giermak says the only time they would withhold
information would be in the case of a potential acquisition or
merger where the acquired company requests confidentiality.

Everett T. Suters, chairman of three Atlanta-based companies and author of *Succeed in Spite of Yourself* (Van Nostrand
Reinhold Co.), says that CEOs who fail to keep their employees
informed about how their company is doing could be making a
big mistake.[1]

Suters relates the following eye-opening experience which
taught him the value of open communication in a company.

He had organized a company that was growing quickly,
requiring long hours from both him and his managers.
Soon, he began to hear rumblings of discontent from
down below, so he called a meeting.

Meetings don't always produce answers, but this one did.

Suters learned that the managers thought they were doing a lot of work for very little credit and less money. His reaction was to ask each manager to write down how much they thought the company was making and how much they thought he was taking out of the coffers.

The chairman found both figures far too high, so he passed out the organization's financial statement and went over it item by item. He then added figures on how much the company needed to earn and what it would take from everybody involved to get there.

His people responded in ways he had not anticipated. He said, "...the more light I shed on the company, the more information I got back in return. In our management meetings and on a casual basis, people were losing their inhibitions about speaking up, and I was getting very useful feedback. It seemed to confirm the old law of physics that for every action there is an opposite and equal reaction."

He found his managers exhibiting more enthusiasm and assuming more responsiblities in the company. He learned they were more motivated because they knew what was going on and how they fit into the overall picture.

"I've found...that almost without exception employees who are kept posted, and feel as if they have a stake in the business, work even harder when all is not going well," Suters said. "...the more open you are, the more responsibility your people will take on. And the more committed they'll feel to you and your organization."

Suters must be managing well. He started one of his companies more than thirty years ago and nearly fifty percent of his current employees have been with the organization more than fifteen years.[2]

The management in some organizations seem to think that their strategic plan must be closely guarded. My experience, again, has shown that such secrecy is wasted effort. Carl R. Heinz, president of Joy Technologies Mining Machinery Group agrees. "You could probably send a copy of your strategic plan directly to all of your competitors and they wouldn't know what to do with it or how to respond."

Once your strategy team has wrestled with the issue of what to share and what to withhold, you can make decisions about what methods you will use to communicate with your people.

And, How Will You Tell Them?

I've broken initial strategy communication methods into three categories. You will want to consider your company and your employees when choosing how you will share important information throughout the ranks.

(1) **Formal/mass communication.** This type of communication goes out to all employees in the form of a printed brochure or document, in-house newsletter articles, video presentations and communication centers or bulletin boards.

(2) **Formal/person-to-person.** Some companies hold a formal kick-off communication event that includes meetings with all employees at which the chief executive makes a presentation. This type communication could also include special branch or department meetings, the use of video presentations, slide shows or other audio/visual media and the distribution of printed material.

The management of First Seneca Bank in Oil City, Pennsylvania, used this technique. They scheduled all-employee meetings in various geographic areas of the service territory. Company president Leonard M. Carroll spoke at every meeting. In addition to Carroll's presentation, a professionally prepared video tape was shown so that all employees would get the same message. Also the group at each meeting was broken into sub-groups which discussed ways they could support the corporate strategy and implement it in their area of responsibility.

Getting employees to participate in introduction of and planning to implement a new strategy is an effective technique for gaining their commitment to the plan.

A similar approach was taken by The Barnes Group. Chairman Wally Barnes and President Bill Fenoglio personally visited every division in the company to communicate the company's guiding philosophy. As Bill describes it:

"We developed the Guiding Philosophy as the common thread so that all of our operations could get under the same umbrella. We feel good about the Guiding Philosophy, because it has a lasting character to it.

The true test of anything is how well you use it, how strongly you believe in it, and how effectively it is communicated one, two and three years after it is developed.

We have primed the pump by starting off with all employee communications meetings where we communicate the strategy, review previous years results, talk about the specific operation that we are visiting, and bring the corporate message.

We have done it every year for three years in a row, and we are dedicated to doing it every year. It's a good way to make sure everybody is rowing the boat in the same cadence."

(3) **Informal or grapevine.** In my strategy sessions, I encourage the top executive team to consider the grapevine and how they can use it to effectively communicate strategy. Even when top-level executives are aware of their company's grapevine, they often do not know how to access it for information or to feed information into it.

In times of crisis, rumors abound. When there are no official answers, no one appears to be in charge. Too often, employees get their company's news from the television at six o'clock. Some organizations have dealt with employee communication during crises by setting up an in-house hotline to provide workers with correct and updated information.

Early in my career when I was involved in employee communication at Joy Manufacturing, we did an assessment of the company grapevine and learned that in our case the old adage, "If you want to know what is going on at the office, check with the town barber," was true. A lot of conversation was taking place in barber shops, beauty shops, churches and other places where people gather.

We decided that the best way to use the Joy grapevine was to make sure that those sites in the community had good information. We sent a copy of the company newsletter to every barber, beautician and clergyman in town.

And, Keep Telling Them?

Necessary communication doesn't stop with the initial imparting of information on company strategy. To keep everybody in touch and on board the company bandwagon, you have to keep throwing the company line out. It can be done on a mass level through organizational newsletters, banners and bulletin boards.

I find that companies that are good at getting the first word out are usually also pretty good at keeping the word going. Joy has a monthly event called "Job Talk."

"Job Talk" is defined as a planned conversation between supervisors and their subordinates. Every month, every supervisor in the company conducts a half-hour meeting to discuss company performance and to collect feedback from employees.

To prepare them for their meetings, supervisors receive a "supervisor's fact sheet," which is a short bulletin listing specific factual information such as sales performance, product shipments and profitability. The fact sheet also includes organizational changes, the current employment picture and other information relevant to company performance.

Supervisors supplement the fact sheet information with items about departmental performance, personnel tidbits and their own observations.

The "Job Talk" format allows for two-way communication. At the conclusion of the event, supervisors fill out a "communication feedback report," which summarizes the comments, questions or suggestions brought up during the "Job Talk." The feedback report is passed back up through the organization and acted on, as appropriate, at each level of management.

The reports eventually land on the desk of the communication coordinator, who summarizes the feedback coming from all across the organization for executive management. Joy's "Job Talks" have proved an excellent way to continually reinforce company strategy and to get feedback from employees about what works and what does not.

Joy has two other techniques for involving employees with other stakeholders that have proved effective in reinforcing Joe Worker's commitment to the company's Strategic Focus. They involve low-level employees in events that most companies would reserve for top executives.

Joy, you will recall, makes mining equipment. Every four years the American Mining Congress holds its Coal Show, a major trade show displaying underground mining machinery. Joy sends the union shop committee members to the show to see the exhibits, check out competitors' equipment displays and talk to customers. Some years the company has included all the employees in the event by producing a video of the committee members at the show, which also, of course, provides a first-hand report of competitors' wares and customers' wants.

Joy also makes a special effort to get as many workers as possible underground in mines to see their machinery in operation and to talk first-hand with customers who use the equipment. These workers return to the factory and share their experience through the "Job Talks." This on-site experience, company management believes, reinforces communication of organization strategy.

Education and Training Play Reinforcing Roles

Many leading companies in this country reinforce organizational strategy through education and training programs. IBM, Xerox, McDonald's and Walt Disney Studios are examples of large companies that run management-development programs within their organizations.

Dana Corporation, a leading manufacturer of components for the control and transmission of power, operates Dana University adjacent to its corporate headquarters in Toledo, Ohio. The university offers both formal and informal education programs aimed at communicating the corporation's strategy. I had the good fortune to spend some time early in my career on the staff at Dana University conducting management-education programs in the fundamentals of supervision, leadership and communication. Dana also offers highly specialized courses in financial management, sales and marketing.

One of Dana's unique characteristics is the executive visit. The organization's focus is "Productivity Through People," and the executive visits demonstrate that the company is serious about its people philosophy. Every class that goes through Dana U spends several hours with one of the organization's top ten or fifteen corporate executives. An executive visits each class group to discuss what is happening in the company and to answer questions in open forum.

Larry Lottier, a long time Dana employee, is now the Dean of the Business School at Dana University. According to Larry, "Our mission is to communicate the 'Dana Style of Management.'

These executive visits give our managers and supervisors a chance to hear first hand how top executives view the Dana Philosophy."

Dana also conducts informal monthly "discussion groups" for young executives-in-training. The groups provide an opportunity for young management people to gain first-hand knowledge from senior executives of the company. A senior executive meets with the group and discusses his or her Dana experience and career path, then responds to questions from the trainees.

Dahlkemper's Leads the Pack in Communicating Strategy

When Dahlkemper's, the catalog showroom chain, entered the marketplace more than thirty years ago, they were the leading low-priced competitors in retailing. Since the late 70s, catalog showrooms have not been able to sustain a competitive advantage through low prices. Dahlkemper's didn't give up and go home; they dealt with the changing market by shifting their focus from low price to customer service (never losing sight of keeping prices competitive). Let's look at several programs the company has incorporated into their strategy:

(1) Customer awareness begins Day 1 at Dahlkemper's. Every new employee must attend a four-hour orientation program before going on the showroom floor. They're informed of the seven Dahlkemper's customer-service "dimensions:"

  (1) Appearance — appropriate personal dress, grooming and departmental appearance.

  (2) Communication — Interpersonal, oral, non-verbal, written and telephone.

  (3) Empathy — customer recognition, listening, sensitivity and special help.

  (4) Enthusiasm — for company, for job, for customers and co-workers.

  (5) Integrity — Company representation,

sales documentation, and organizational
confidentiality.

(6) Knowledge — of company, of competition
and of products.

(7) Reliability — attendance, initiative,
judgment, follow-up and productivity.

(2) New hires receive The Dahlkemper Difference
Handbook, which stresses the customer-service
dimensions. The seven dimensions with their
multiple elements are built into the
employee-evaluation program. The showroom
manager gives A-1 Awards to employees who
demonstrate a high level of customer and
co-worker awareness, and Joseph Dahlkemper, who
manages by wandering around, makes a big issue of
awarding highly valued "Gold Bee" pins to
employees who have demonstrated exceptional
performance in customer awareness.

(3) Dahlkemper's customer service awareness is not
concentrated among the front-line salespeople. It's
a company-wide focus. The company has
developed training programs that help staff link
their jobs to customer satisfaction. For example,
corporate merchandisers are given special training
in writing fact tags. Company management believes
the fact tag serves as a silent sales tool for the
customer who wants information about a product
but prefers not to approach a salesperson on the
showroom floor.

(4) The strategy is carried a step further through
training managers in the personnel interviewing
and selection process. Since customer awareness is a
critical element for hiring, managers must be able
to recruit and select people who will give superior
service. Managers are taught behavioral
interviewing techniques so that the questions used
in an interview will help them predict the behavior

style of each applicant and to place personnel where they will be most effective.

(5) Dahlkemper's OSCAR Award was developed to reinforce understanding and implementation of the corporate strategy. The acronym OSCAR stands for "Obstacles to Serving Customers Are Removable." The OSCAR, a large toy truck mounted on a plaque, is a traveling award given to the person who removes most obstacles to serving customers.

(6) The company's "Adopt-a-Showroom" program has also been effective in communicating the customer-service strategy. Each officer in the corporation selects a showroom in which he or she will spend considerable time reinforcing corporate philosophy. For example, the chief financial officer may spend several days a month in a chosen showroom waiting on customers, working at the checkout station or helping in the warehouse. Benefits of the "Adopt-a-Showroom" program go several directions. Customers and salespeople benefit, of course, from management's involvement, and the officers return to their strategy-planning sessions with a clearer understanding of life on the front line.

(7) Still another successful Dahlkemper practice is their product-training program. They offer specialized "courses" in many of the items they sell. An example is the grandfather clock seminar, in which the training coordinator goes onto the showroom floor with a small group of salespeople. They all gather around one of the grandfather clocks while the coordinator gives a detailed explanation of how the big guys work and how to sell them. Wouldn't you know! The activity draws a group of interested customers and invariably results in a couple of sales of the expensive item. Dahlkemper's astute training coordinators are well aware that training sessions

on the sales floor have such a positive impact on customer perceptions.

Dahlkemper's combination of new-employee orientation, customer-awareness skills and product knowledge, reinforced by their Gold Bees and OSCARS, has gone a long way to make customer awareness and service an integral part of the way the company does business.

A Good Ad Campaign Can Be the Key to Success

Creative advertising is an effective technique for communicating corporate strategy both to the public and to your employees.

When Avis Rent-a-Car management realized they needed to make a move, they didn't plan a strategy and quietly keep it under wraps; they broadcast it to the world. "Here's our plan. Stop us if you can." The company's technique is considered an advertising classic.

When Bob Townsend took over Avis, they were struggling in the marketplace and losing money. Townsend had no experience in rental cars; he was a people person, having come out of the American Express organization. He huddled and strategized with his marketing and advertising people and they came up with the "We're # 2, we try harder" campaign.

Years after the move, Townsend admits that the ad campaign probably did more for Avis employees than for Avis customers. True, the company quickly went from the #5 or #6 position to the #2 slot, but customers also acknowledged that Avis employees really did try harder and that service gave them the competitive advantage.

We saw a similar example in Lee Iacocca's success at Chrysler Motors.

When Iacocca took over, Chrysler was in deep financial trouble and lacked a Strategic Focus. After getting some money from the federal government to keep the company afloat, Iacocca embarked on a major quality program. He initiated the five-year/50,000-mile warranty and went on national television to personally promote Chrysler products and Chrysler quality.

The company rebounded quickly, increased its sales and recovered financially. Again, Chrysler's advertising did as much for its employees as it did for the car-buying public. The workers bought in; they were part of the new Strategic Focus. They believed in it.

Ford did it too. They got their people on the company wagon with their "Quality Is Job-1" program. The company put a great deal of in-house effort toward developing and communicating their Strategic Focus, then used the slogan in their external advertising. The advertising reinforced employee support as much as it caught buyers' attention.

The organization would have wasted its time and money advertising quality if they could not provide it in the bays — that's why the rank and file has to buy in to make a strategy work. This broader effect is one which organizations should take into consideration when developing an advertising campaign. Not only does a good advertising plan promote and sell products, it can also be an effective tool for communicating with employees.

You've Got to Show You Mean It

In this chapter, I have tried to identify some specific techniques that companies can use to communicate their strategies and philosophies, but communication alone is not enough. Demonstrating that you mean what you say is also important. Chet Giermak of Eriez says it best:

The best way to communicate our philosophy is to show people that we really believe in that philosophy. We hire people who believe the philosophy. We provide safe, clean working conditions. We give our customers real value. We pay our people the area average or better. We removed all of the timeclocks. We shared profits with everyone every year, long before profit-sharing was common. We created noncontributory pension plans long before that was common. We're good neighbors in the community and we work hard to make our community a better place to live.

All this leads to a company that has no problem finding people to represent it in the field or to work in the factory. We put people ahead of profits. We get awfully good people and very good profits.

KEY POINTS

(1) Every person in an organization must understand and be committed to making Strategic Focus happen.

(2) When an entire organization identifies with the mission, there is virtually no limit to what you can do.

(3) The two chief divisions in communicating Strategic Focus are the initial introduction and on-going information about corporate strategy.

(4) CEOs who fail to keep their employees informed about how their company is doing make a big mistake.

(5) Necessary communication doesn't stop with the initial imparting of information on company strategy. You have to keep throwing the company line out.

(6) Creative advertising is an effective technique for communicating corporate strategy both to the public and to your employees.

(7) Communication alone is not enough. Demonstrating that you mean what you say is also important.

NOTES:

[1] Everett T. Suters, *"Show and Tell,"* INC., (April, 1987), pp. 111-112.

[2] Ibid.

CHAPTER TEN

The Strategy Diamond™ - A Model for Implementation

PURPOSE: *To present a visual model and some hands-on techniques that can be used in implementing your Strategic Focus.*

If strategic focusing is to bear fruit, it must be hauled down from the rhetorical ivory tower and implemented through consistent daily execution.

Fran Tarkenton, former Minnesota Vikings quarterback, who since retirement from football has transferred his gridiron management knowledge to the workplace, says:

If football taught me anything about business, it is that you win the game one play at a time....don't go for 15 risky yards when you can get 5 sure ones. It is a principle of the marketplace that you will never fail if you take your gains modestly but consistently....

When in doubt, remember that in football an 80-yard drive is better than an 80-yard "bomb." The bomb — the long pass that scores a touchdown — can be dismissed by the other team as a lucky, one-time fluke, which it probably is. The sustained drive that systematically pushes the other team back over its own goal line shows them that you play sound, unbeatable football, and is far more demoralizing to your opposition.[1]

Tarkenton's advice is as appropriate for the board room as it is on the football field. Businesses that find themselves in a lucky situation where they grow by leaps and bounds and go for the long bomb are far fewer than the ones that are able to sustain modest, yet consistent growth. It pays to develop and implement corporate strategy that resembles Tarkenton's 80-yard drive.

THE STRATEGY DIAMOND™

Over the past ten years I have helped probably a hundred different organizations create vision and develop strategy, using the process described earlier. Creating the vision is hard work, but turning it into reality is the harder part. Implementation of strategy is the key.

Many of my clients have been frustrated by not putting their strategies into action as quickly or as effectively as they would like. To help them, I have spent hundreds of hours collecting information and thinking about the process of implementation. The result is a model I call The Strategy Diamond ™

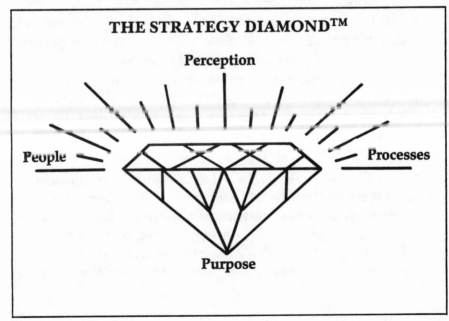

THE STRATEGY DIAMOND™

Perception

People   Processes

Purpose

The symbol of the diamond represents excellent organizations. Like the diamond, they are rare, multi-faceted and beautiful. By putting into practice the twenty elements of The Strategy Diamond™ you can create an organization that is a real gem in the marketplace.

The elements of The Strategy Diamond™ are divided into four dimensions: Purpose, People, Processes and Perception.

In our model, Purpose is at the point of the diamond. There is some symbolism there. If people get the "point" of what you are trying to accomplish, they will help you get there.

On the sides of the diamond are two dimensions that are closely linked together, People and Processes. The top of the diamond is the part that you see in jewelry, and that represents Perception. The value of a gem is determined by how it is perceived by the wearer and is measured by the four C's — **C**ut, **C**larity, **C**olor and **C**arat weight. The value of the organization is measured by the perception by various stakeholder groups.

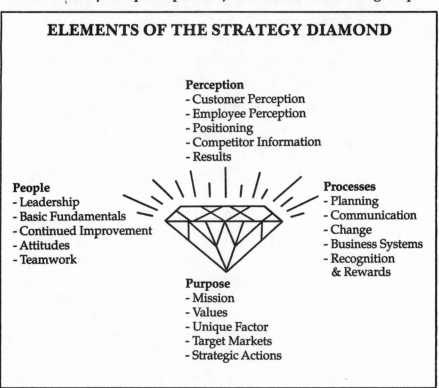

ELEMENTS OF THE STRATEGY DIAMOND

Perception
- Customer Perception
- Employee Perception
- Positioning
- Competitor Information
- Results

People
- Leadership
- Basic Fundamentals
- Continued Improvement
- Attitudes
- Teamwork

Processes
- Planning
- Communication
- Change
- Business Systems
- Recognition
  & Rewards

Purpose
- Mission
- Values
- Unique Factor
- Target Markets
- Strategic Actions

We have divided the four phases into twenty elements. Each of these basic elements can be defined, created and observed in your organization. The twenty elements are:

Purpose
- Mission
- Values
- Unique Factor

- Target Markets
- Strategic Actions

People
- Leadership
- Basic Fundamentals

- Continual Improvement
- Attitudes
- Teamwork

Processes
- Planning
- Communication
- Change Management

- Business Systems
- Recognition and Reward

Perception
- Customer Perception
- Employee Perception

- Positioning
- Competitor Information
- Results

Let's look at each of these elements in a little more detail.

PURPOSE

Mission In an earlier chapter, we talked about the process of defining the mission of your business. Knowing what your business is, and what it is not, are critically important. That same thing is true for departments, divisions and individuals.

Many times, the planning process in a company begins with some kind of mission statement. Seldom do we find departments or divisions that have a clearly written mission, and almost never do individual employees have their own personal mission statements.

The importance of this was reinforced for me several years ago. I was conducting a seminar on management planning and control for a large public utility company. As part of the program, I had the participants write mission statements for their own jobs using a worksheet I had developed. At the end of the day, a young computer specialist came up and thanked me for making such an impact on his thinking. "But," he said, "the bad news is that I have to go back to my boss and try to renegotiate my objectives for the year."

When I asked why, he said that he had written his objectives based on tasks to be accomplished. As an outcome of the seminar and his own mission statement, he realized that he needed to focus on results rather than activities. He had suddenly gotten the point of what his job is all about.

Values Nothing is more vital to the implementation of corporate strategy than a top executive team that lives and breathes the guiding philosophy. It's not enough just to have a strategy and a philosophy; it's top management who must translate the philosophy into reality.

> —It's Chet Giermak, who for more than twenty-eight years has walked through the Eriez Magnetics shop every day he was in town saying "Hi" to every employee. Eriez's philosophy: "We put people before profits."

> —It's Walt Disney, who strolled the Disneyland and Walt Disney World theme parks talking with ride operators and ticket takers, recognizing employees who exhibited the Disney attitude and giving feedback to those who didn't smile quite the way he thought they should.

> —It's Sam Walton, chairman of Walmart Stores, who spends sixty percent of his time in the field visiting each of his 1200+ stores every year.

— It's Joy Technologies sending factory workers into underground coal mines around the country so they will more clearly understand the job of the miner.

— It's Ren McPherson, former chairman of the Dana Corporation, who spent large portions of his time visiting the organization's plants and talking to the people about his philosophy of "Productivity Through People."

Living the corporate philosophy carries on into top management decision making. In two instances, I had chief executives of different companies tell me similar stories about the importance of using their corporate strategy in making day-to-day operating decisions.

Joseph B. Dahlkemper, president of the J.B. Dahlkemper Company, and Carl R. Heinz, president of the Mining Machinery Group of Joy Technologies, each told of sitting in a meeting in which a group of key executives were discussing a major decision. In both instances, the chief executive realized that the strategic plan would provide guidance in making the decisions in question, yet none of the operating executives recalled having had a similar discussion during strategy-setting meetings. In each case, when a copy of the strategic plan was produced, it was clear that the document held the answers to their questions. The decision about how to handle the situation had been made during the Executive Strategy Retreat.

One of the big challenges I see for top executive groups is to develop the practice of using strategy and values to guide thinking on a daily basis.

John Findley, president of Findley Adhesives in Milwaukee, Wisconsin, helped his people put together a guiding philosophy statement they call their corporate credo. Findley said the company felt a need for a guideline that applied to everyone in the organization at any time.

I wanted the guys in the shipping department at three o'clock in the morning debating about whether or not to send out a Findley product in a ratty old box or to go get a new one to have a basis for making that decision. We wanted a strategy statement that would make sense to everybody from the chairman to the guy who sweeps out the loading dock at night.

It's not only necessary that everybody from the chairman to the sweeper understand the philosophy, but that they accept it and put it into action.

Unique Factor Critically important to the implementation of your Strategic Focus is your unique factor. Only when every one in the organization understands what makes you unique, can they help to make that uniqueness real.

What makes McDonald's unique? Consistency. They do it the same way every time. What makes IBM unique? Service. They vow to give the best service of any company in the world. What makes Walt Disney World unique? Cleanliness and courtesy. They are fanatical about keeping the place clean.

To be successful in implementing your Strategic Focus, you must have a clearly defined Unique Factor, which is the basis for your competitive advantage. You must concentrate your efforts on strengthening that Unique Factor, so that you clearly differentiate yourself from your competitors.

Target Markets The biggest barrier to organizations achieving their Strategic Focus is trying to be all things to all people. This is especially true when companies try to be all things to all customers. The surest route to strategic success in the marketplace is to focus on specific selected target markets.

You must clearly define the target markets you will choose to serve. Then you must clearly understand the needs and wants of customers in those selected market segments. This will help everyone in the organization set priorities on how to allocate time, dollars and other resources. This focus on target markets also makes it much easier to create the desired position in the minds of the customers. Customers prefer to deal with companies that specialize in their industry, just like patients prefer to use a physician who specializes in their particular illness or injury.

There is plenty of evidence to suggest that companies and individuals who focus on specific target markets are more profitable than generalists. Physicians, attorneys and accountants who specialize are able to charge higher fees. Companies that specialize are able to charge higher prices, and gain cost advantage due to economies of scale. they can also gain marketing advantage due to the cumulative effect of advertising and promotion. Selecting specific target markets makes implementing your Strategic Focus much easier.

Strategic Actions Having a strategy in writing is one thing. Turning it into true competitive advantage is quite another. The key is action. What are you going to do to gain competitive action?

Strategic actions are those things you will do to gain and sustain competitive advantage in the marketplace. They involve major projects that prepare the organization for competition.

The way to define strategic actions is to define the basic fundamentals of the business. Then assess the strengths and weaknesses of the organization in terms of mastering those fundamentals, and determine what action seems appropriate.

In our work with executive strategy teams, we find that the strategic actions they develop often fall into the other three phases of the Strategy Diamond™. For example, many of our clients have developed strategic actions that relate to people. They might include human resource planning, training and development, or team building. Strategic actions may relate to processes, such as the planning process, communication, recognition and rewards, or actions involving changing business systems. In the area of perceptions, strategic actions often relate to measuring customer perception or employee perception, gathering competitive information, or developing systems to measure results on a more timely and accurate basis.

The secret is not to have so many Stratgic Actions that they contribute to lack of focus. You want to concentrate on those actions that are going to have the greatest impact on the organization's ability to compete in the marketplace. That is why a hard, introspective look at strengths and weaknesses is so important.

One way I judge how effectively the strategy team is doing with strengths and weaknesses is to look at the length and specificity of the lists. If they have a long and specific list of strengths but a short general list of weaknesses, I am concerned that they are not being honest with themselves. If, on the other hand, there is a long list of specific weaknesses that have to be addressed, that suggests rather honest appraisal was made.

Concentrating on fixing the weaknesses is not necessary in developing strategic actions. But you had better know what they are. If you are having trouble identifying weaknesses, go ask your middle managers and front line supervisors. They'll help you see them.

Often, organizations I work with end up with two or three strategic actions that affect the whole organization, and then one or two in each functional area. For example, the organization may have an overall action to improve product quality or customer service. Perhaps there is a strategic action to communicate the mission and strategy to the organization. Then, the Human Resources Department may have a strategic action to develop a human resource planning system, or to develop training programs to support the strategy. Finance may have an action to upgrade the management information system to provide more timely information on the Critical Measures of Success.

The important thing is that these strategic actions are specific and doable. People have to see that a plan is in place to make the organization more effective.

PEOPLE

Leadership Dwight D. Eisenhower, head of the Allied troops during World War II and thirty-fourth President of the United States, expressed the philosophy that "leadership is the art of getting someone else to do something that you want done because he wants to do it." Eisenhower is reported to have demonstrated the art of good management or leadership by comparing the effect of pushing a rope ineffectively around on a table or pulling it directly to his goal.

A pushed rope won't push back, but people sometimes will. There's no progress in that situation. Involved, committed people who are focused on a mission can be led wherever you want them to go.

Your top management team must lead by example. They must have a clear vision for the organization, and their actions must consistently support and reinforce the vision and strategy. It is important that leaders do not send mixed signals.

For example, if your company has in place a performance management system involving performance objectives, quarterly reviews, and an annual performance appraisal, the top executives must make the system work. I have middle managers say to me, "How can I set my performance objectives if my boss hasn't done his yet?" Developing programs and procedures for the lower levels in the organization is useless if the top executives don't set the example. Actions speak louder than words. How does that popular old saying go? "What you do speaks so loudly I cannot hear what you say."

Basic Fundamentals Mastering the basic fundamentals of the business is essential to implementing Strategic Focus. The first step is to define these basic fundamentals. Next you must create systems so the fundamentals can be repeated over and over again. Finally, you must provide training to give your people the basic skills needed to perform these fundamentals.

Let's use our old friends at the golden arches as an example. The Unique Factor at McDonald's is consistency. No matter where you go in the world, a Big Mac looks and tastes like a Big Mac. The basic fundamentals of building this popular sandwich are raw materials, cooking, assembly, and

packaging. First, you must find a supplier of raw materials
that will provide consistent quality. Next you must develop a
recipe for the sauce, and design the little foam box. Then you
must teach the griddle person the proper steps to prepare
and cook the all beef patty. You must systematize this whole
process so that every store in the chain does it the very same
way.

That is the success secret of companies like McDonald's,
Marriott, Delta Airlines and others. Define the fundamentals
of making the product or serving the customer. Then develop processes and people skills to repeat those fundamentals flawlessly over and over again.

NCNB National Bank makes a lot of news. They're for-
ever buying up or merging with or "rescuing" other financial
organizations. They go for the eighty-yard bomb. On the
other hand, competitor, Wachovia Bank and Trust Co., also
a North Carolina institution, is sedate and quiet — and
secure. Wachovia just moves along at a steady pace, making
first downs. And year after year, polls of leading banking
officers in the country vote Wachovia's management the most
reputable and stable on the national scene.

Nido Qubein, a management consultant whom I mentioned earlier, talks about managing the macro and the micro
features of an organization. Very often, failure to manage the
macro, the big things, isn't what kills you, Qubein notes. It's
failure to manage the micro, the little details.

Continual Improvement Being good enough today is not good
enough. You must constantly strive to get better. If you don't,
your competitors will. There are many classic stories in
"Chapter Eleven" of companies who failed to improve. They
got comfortable with their position in the marketplace, and
stopped doing what made them successful in the first place.

First, people must want to improve. Then, they must have
the opportunity. And finally, there must be some incentive.
The first part is no problem. Most workers we know have an
innate desire to make things better. It is called "constructive

dissatisfaction with the status quo." They don't like it the way it is, and they want to make it better.

Opportunity can be a real problem. Workers recognize that there is a problem or an opportunity to improve. They make a suggestion to their supervisor. The supervisor doesn't respond. Or the supervisor goes to the general foreman with the idea, but the general foreman doesn't respond. Nothing happens. The employee makes another suggestion for improvement. Still nothing happens. Finally the employee says to himself, "If they don't care, why should I care." As a result, you keep on doing the same thing wrong over and over again until one day your competitor figures out a better way to do it and takes your customer away.

Given the willingness and the opportunity, the third piece of continual improvement is providing some incentive to improve. At Dana Corporation, a number of plants operate under the Scanlon Plan. Employee participation teams identify problems and work out solutions. Productivity is measured against a base line, using Total Sales Per Employee as the measure. If productivity goes up as a result of the improvement, every employee in the plant receives a bonus.

At Creative Pultrusions, Bob Sweet has created a group incentive program based on profitability. One-third of pre-tax profits are put into a bonus fund and distributed to all employess. A point system using position level, seniority and performance is used to allocate the dollars. You can believe that every employee in that plant is looking for opportunities for continual improvement, because improvement in the plant means improvement in profit, which means increases in bonus pay.

Attitudes Attitudes are habits of thought. Those patterns of thinking get translated into action on the job. If people have attitudes that are positive and cheerful, their actions on the job are positive and helpful. If people have attitudes that are negative, their behavior gets in the way of serving the customer or cooperating with co-workers.

There's a story making the management rounds about

the customer in the department store who watched in amazement as a grumpy sales clerk treated another customer in a surly and unpleasant manner. When the clerk turned to her with the same unhappy attitude and said, "May I help you?" she said, "No, young man. You have it wrong. Let me help you. I represent income. You represent overhead."

Enthusiasm for an organization is not infectious like dissatisfaction is. People don't just automatically get excited about a mission or the company's Strategic Focus. Individuals like to be a part of success and a successful operation and are receptive to ideas that will create enthusiasm, but their natural tendency is to find fault and to look for excuses why things won't work. Consequently, kindling enthusiasm has to be a positive, concerted effort on the part of management in order for it to trickle down through the ranks. Management has to constantly inoculate the organization with enthusiasm and the inoculation has to take. Employees have to buy into the enthusiasm.

If you've visited one of the Walt Disney theme parks, you have probably noticed that even the young person with a broom and a dust pan has bought into the mission and is a friendly emissary for the organization. And that enthusiasm is catching. If you don't watch out, you'll catch yourself skipping happily along through the park like Dorothy did over Oz's yellow brick road — just because all around you people are smiling.

The same can be true in your company. When management has their mission in mind and their values in view and communicates that purpose to the rest of the organization, everybody else catches the condition. Assembly line workers become more than tap tightners and sole stitchers; they become car builders and shoe makers. The company becomes more than Ford Motor Company or Buster Brown Shoes, they become "my" car company and "my" shoe factory. There is no mission or strategy unless everyone in the organization knows it and understands it.

J. Willard Marriott and his wife, Allie, were known for their ability to instill enthusiasm in their people in the Marriott chain of businesses. They concentrated on promoting good will both with their employees and their customers. They often visited the stores, walked through the work area and talked with the help. And they mingled with customers, introduced themselves and asked what the patrons liked or did not like about the food or the service. This attitude of concern for the customer has been conveyed to thousands of Marriott employees around the world, and has made the company a leader in the hospitality industry.[2]

Teamwork Teamwork is a group of people, working in an environment of mutual trust and respect, striving toward a common goal. A true high performing team has a mystical sense of camaraderie and mutual support. Excellent communication takes place, often in an unspoken, almost intuitive manner.

There are zillions of examples of teamwork we could discuss. The one that comes to mind for me is the crew of a sailing ship. Several years ago I conducted an Executive Strategy Retreat for a client aboard The Schooner *Roseway*. The *Roseway* is a 134foot woodenmasted ship sailing out of Camden, Maine. We boarded the ship on a Wednesday evening, and sailed Penobscot Bay for five days. We worked in the morning, sailed in the afternoon, and then had more meetings in the evening. It was an excellent site for a retreat.

While we were sailing, I observed the teamwork of the captain and crew of the *Roseway*. They agreed on our destination, mapped out a course, and then worked together as one to sail the ship. They used the executive team on board for muscle to raise and lower the sails. The rest of the work was done by four young deck hands. These young people went about their work with precision and grace. Because of the wind, verbal communication was difficult, yet each seemed to know what the other was going to do, and when. Not only did this crew demonstrate the element of teamwork, but many of the other elements of Strategic Focus.

PROCESSES

Planning Much of this book has dealt with planning, so I won't spend a lot of time elaborating. Having a process for planning is important. It should be a circular process that repeats itself, preferrably every year. The planning process should be linked to the annual budgeting cycle. Linking planning to other processes, such as communication, and recognition and rewards, is also helpful.

Communication We have also spent many pages talking about the need for communication, and some techniques for communicating your strategy. The point here is that you should have in place a process for communicating. The process begins with What you want to communicate. Then it should address Who you want to communicate with, When you want to communicate, and How.

    When I was at the Dana Corporation in the late 70's, every manager at the corporate office had a small TV on his desk. Any information the manager wanted about the operation of the business was available on one of the channels of the TV. One channel had an ongoing news program. It constantly scrolled company news, the current stock price, and major economic and business news from around the world. It was also a place to tell employees about the next company softball game, the employees association racquetball and pizza party, or other items of local interest. TV monitors placed in public areas of the office were tuned to this news channel.

    At First Seneca Bank, in Oil City, Pennsylvania, they have developed a system of interbranch communications that enables them to get relevant information to all employees in all branches simultaneously. This was particularly helpful when the bank went through several mergers, and wanted to inform all employees at once, rather than to have them read the news in the local paper.

    Joy Technologies has a program called "Job Talks" to communicate with employees. A "Job Talk" is a planned conversation between a supervisor and his or her people. Every supervisor in Joy's Franklin, Pennsylvania, operation spends at least thirty minutes a month in a "Job Talk", passing on company performance information and organization news, and collecting feedback from employees. The feedback is collected, summarized and passed on to senior management to help them keep their finger on the pulse of employee perception.

Regardless of what system you use, having a system is important. One to one informal communication and "management by wandering around" are great, but having a more formal process to get timely information to employees and to collect feedback from them is also necessary.

Change Management The business world as we know it is in a state of constant change. You can make change happen, or you can let it happen to you. The companies with a clear sense of Strategic Focus recognize that they must manage change, and they put in place processes to make that happen. A systematic process for managing strategic change can be an important tool for moving your company into the future.

The biggest problem with most change management processes is that they view change from one perspective — that of the designer. The person making the change looks at it from his or her perspective only.

My friend and colleague Carl Heinz and I have been working on a change management model that has two parallel paths. One path looks at change from the designer perspective. The other looks at it from the user perspective. Users go through a series of steps in response to any change. First is awareness. Then comes personal concern. How will this change affect me personally? Next is mechanical concern. How will this new thing work? What are the mechanics of it? Finally is concern for the consequences. How will this new change affect the company, the customer or the people?

Having in place a process to manage change that takes into account both the designer perspective and the user perspective is an important part of implementing your strategy. Many of the business fads that boomed and then went bust didn't take user concern into account. Sound concepts like MBO, Quality Circles and Strategic Planning have failed in many companies because those companies didn't have in place a process to manage the change required to make these ideas work.

Major changes in an organization will probably be disliked initially. A manager has to decide whether to take the negative attitude as an objection or a contribution. Consider this scenario:

> Your organization is facing a major system change on a production line. You're going from manual to computer control of a procedure. So you get with your supervisor to discuss the change.

> Jones immediately voices concern about reduced productivity. You respond, "You're probably right; I think we will have a loss of productivity. How low do you think it will go before it bottoms out?"

> Jones is surprised that you did not argue with him or just tell him flat out that with the extra equipment expense, the company certainly can't stand reduced production too.

> His attitude turns positive. "Oh, I expect we could bottom out in about two weeks," he calculates.

> You go to your flipchart and quickly sketch a graph with time across the top and production percentages along the side.

> "Two weeks, you say?" you ask the supervisor, and you go out two weeks and plot a point and draw a line. "Where do you think it will bottom out? About eighty percent? Let's plan on seventy percent just in case. We have a good reputation for shipping our product on time, good loyal customers. If we go below seventy percent production, we can't ship. Is there any way we can hedge that bet and still maintain our relationship with our customers when we switch over to computers?"

> Now Jones is really drawn into the change. He suggests overproduction giving line employees overtime, stockpiling.

"That way, when we can't ship from the line, we can ship from the warehouse, and the customer won't know the difference," the supervisor says. He's focused on keeping up production, solving the problem, and taking the necessary steps to affect the change efficiently. And he goes back and sells his employees on the plan. The way they start cranking up production, you think they're out there singing, "Get on board, Little Children; this train is bound for Glory." They've got a mission. They're the only ones right now who can keep the company on track. And they're getting more attention from upperlevel management than they've had in a long time.

You go back into the plant and hang up your graph where everyone can see it. You hook up the computers and implement a training program, and you're back there every day checking and encouraging and keeping in touch.

Productivity starts down. You mark it on the chart. But that's not depressing. You all expected that. You're prepared.

It's descending — 81%, 80%, 80%, 81%, 82%. It's bottomed out.

You just play it cool. You didn't really think it would go below eighty percent, but workers on the line didn't know that. You have that seventy percent figure up there and they've beaten that by ten percent. Their supervisor looks good. They feel good. What a morale booster!

Ignore the two weeks you were below quota. Ignore the fact that you had to pay big overtime checks to pad the stock. Take advantage of the good news. Announce the achievement plant-wide. "Productivity is up today." "Department C's rate of recovery is ahead of projection," or industry average, or whatever. Celebrate!

Keep your chart going. At some point, you will get back to 100% of your old production. You still won't have any return on investment, but you are on the way. When you cross that 100%-of-old-production line, you can continue to keep spirits high because you are announcing record-breaking figures. You know what you have to reach to pay off investment and start making a profit. Keep focusing on that point on your chart. Keep your workers informed of the figures. When you know they are really committed and putting out, give a free lunch in the cafeteria.

The losses you incurred below the old figures will be offset by the gains above them, and when you reach break-even, celebrate again.

You've managed change effectively. The company is in good shape, and you are probably just about to move another rung up the management ladder.

Richard B. Fisher, Manager of Organization Development and Staffing, and a specialist on managing change with the LORD Corporation in Erie, Pennslyvania, gives the following self-test to check your preparation for initiating a change. Fisher says:

The highest form of commitment to change is internalization. When people have internalized an organizational change, it has become part of their personal creed. Their personal values about it have become aligned with the organization's values.

Business Systems The processes we have discussed so far are soft issues. They are more people oriented than product or numbers oriented. Every successful company must have in place hard systems to run the business. These hard systems include things like financial systems, inventory control, computer assisted manufacturing, and electronically controlled distribution systems. These are systems that are linked to the basic fundamentals of the business.

Our friends at Bowman Products in Cleveland, Ohio, are in the business of supplying maintenance and repair parts to industrial plants, automobile repair shops, and service businesses such as hospitals and hotels. They sell fasteners, cleaning supplies, solvents and other materials that would be used by the maintenance department.

Bowman's Unique Factor is what they call "The Bowman System." This is a unique system of determining the customer's need for maintenance items, setting up inventory control bins, and making sure those bins are never empty. They become more than just a seller of hardware. They become part of the customer's inventory control system. In order for Bowman to keep their customers satisfied, they must have their own sophisticated systems for calling on customers, taking orders, filling those orders, distributing the product to the customer, and putting the product in the customer's storage bins. Each step in this process provides additional value to the customer, and Bowman is able to charge a premium price for those value added services. These processes allow Bowman to serve the customer differently than other suppliers and therefore gain competitive advantage in the marketplace.

Recognition and Reward Motivation is that internal driving force that causes people to take action because they believe that action will benefit them in some way. If we want people to take action that is consistent with the mission and strategy of the company, they must get something of value in return. That value in return can be money or tangible fringe benefits, or it may come in the form of recognition and personal job satisfaction.

A critical process to have in place is a recognition and reward system that is linked to the business strategy. It begins with executive compensation. Top executives should receive bonuses based on how effectively they implement the Strategic Focus and how that affects competitive advantage in the marketplace over a long period of time.

One division of a large corporation that we worked with had developed an effective competitive strategy. They were frustrated by how slowly implementation was going. Investigation revealed that all of the executives on the strategy team had a separate set of objectives that they had submitted to the corporate office for the Management Incentive Compensation Program. Almost all of the MICP goals were tied to shortterm financial performance, rather than the longterm strategy of the business. What do you think they paid attention to the longterm strategy or the shortterm numbers? You got that right! They were concentrating on making this month's numbers even if that meant sacrificing longterm competitive advantage.

Longterm strategy and shortterm results don't have to conflict with one another. But if the system rewards one without the other, you will only get one.

Another important part of this process is some type of merit pay or performance management system for middle managers and supervisors The objectives of this system must be closely linked to the overall goals of the company, so that managers can clearly see how their job and their performance is tied to implementing strategy.

The key here is to make sure you are rewarding the activities that make a real contribution to the implementation of Strategic Focus, and to bottom line results.

PERCEPTION

Customer Perception Every organization we have worked with in Executive Strategy Retreats has identified Customer Satisfaction as one of their Critical Measures of Success, yet few of these companies had in place a system to measure it. Keeping in touch with the customer is critical to strategic success.

There are four methods you can use to get regular and accurate feedback from your customers. Customer satisfaction surveys are paper and pencil or telephone surveys asking your customers to rate you on a number of different dimensions of customer satisfaction. Focus groups are groups of ten to twelve customers who agree to come together to discuss their reaction to your products and services. Letters to the president, if properly collected and tabulated, can be a wonderful source of customer feedback. In some organizations, mystery shopper audits can be used to measure effectiveness in dealing with customers.

Informal methods such as customer visits, customer appreciation days, and executive telephone followup can also be used to keep in touch. Regardless of the method you use, a systematic process is important for collecting, tabulating and responding to customer perception.

Employee Perception Customer relations are a mirror image of employee relations. If your employees are enthusiastic about their jobs and their company, they will pass their enthusiam on to the customer. If your employees are angry or dissatisfied with the company, they will take it out on your customers.

Keeping in touch with the perceptions of your employees is second in importance only to keeping in touch with your customers. There are many ways to do that. Employee attitude surveys, focus groups, feedback from training programs, and informal meetings with the CEO are just a few ways of keeping in touch.

Many companies have done employee attitude surveys. Most make three common mistakes:

1. They don't give feedback to the employees on the findings of the survey;
2. They don't take action on the findings;
3. They don't follow up and repeat the survey to see if anything has changed.

If you are going to do any kind of employee survey, you should commit to do three things:

1. Tell all employees the results of the survey;
2. Tell them what action you are going to take. What are you going to do now? What are you going to do later? What aren't you going to do at all, and why?
3. Repeat the same survey every two years, and compare the results. Measure the progress. Be sure to use the same survey so you can compare apples to apples. Having data from two or three

different surveys only causes confusion about
how employees really view the organization.

Positioning Positioning is the process of creating a clear position
in the mind of your customers for your company or your
product. This is a concept that is used by many advertising
and marketing agencies to help their clients. It was made
popular by Al Ries and Jack Trout in their book, *Positioning,
The Battle for the Mind*[3].

My friend Nido Qubein speaks frequently to business
groups on the subject of positioning. He encourages his
audience to answer three questions: How do you want to be
described by your customers? How do they describe you
now? What is the difference?

The position your company or your product holds in the
mind of the customer is critical to determining your strategic
success. The classic example of conscious positioning is Avis
Rent-a-Car with their campaign, "We're Number Two. We
Try Harder." That position has become so engrained in
people that Payne Stewart, the professional golfer who won
the 1989 PGA Tournament, was nicknamed "Avis" by his
friends on the tour because he came in second so often.

Competitor Information Another key piece of perception is the
perception you have of your competitors. The ability to
gather and interpret accurate information about your competitors is a critical part of positioning yourself in the marketplace.

Too often, when you talk to executives about their competitors, they tend to put them down. They talk in negative
terms. They don't take their competitors seriously.

Companies with clear Strategic Focus spend considerable
time and energy gathering information about their competitors. Stew Leonard, the now famous proprietor of Stew
Leonards Dairy in Norwalk, Connecticut, makes a practice
of taking groups of his employees on scouting trips into other
stores. When they return they sit down and talk about what
they observed. There is only one rule: "You can't talk about
what we do better than they do. You can only talk about what

the competitor does better." This keen observation of the competitor's strengths forces a focus on continual improvement.

Results The final element in our list of twenty is results. The surest way to measure the perception of your customers, your employees and your competitors is through bottom line results. Growth in sales, market share and profitability are sure indicators that you are doing something right.

We left this element for last for a reason. It is our philosophical belief that results follow focus. If you do all of the other things correctly in running your business, positive financial results will follow. I'm not suggesting that profits aren't important. I'm just saying that they come naturally if you have paid attention to the other details of running the business.

KEY POINTS

(1) **Three yards and a cloud of dust is better than a long bomb in football and in business.**

(2) **The Strategy Diamond™ is divided into four phases: Purpose, People, Processes and Perception.**

(3) **Each of the twenty elements can be defined, created and observed in your company.**

(4) **These twenty elements are the fundamentals of implementing Strategic Focus.**

NOTES:

[1] As quoted in Robert W. Keidel, *Game Plans* (New York: E.P.Dutton), pp. 12-13.

[2] Robert O'Brien, *Marriott* (Salt Lake City, Utah: Deseret Book Company, 1978), p. 137.

[3] Al Ries & Jack Trout, *Positioning: The Battle For Your Mind* (New York: McGraw-Hill, 1981).

How to Keep Your Focus in Focus

PURPOSE: *To emphasize the importance of measuring customer satisfaction and demonstrate how to measure it more satisfactorily. We'll also talk about how to guide the execution of your Strategic Focus.*

Most companies measure sales, cash flow, costs, productivity and many other "vital signs" to monitor their corporate health. But very few systematically monitor their customers' perceptions, expectations and satisfaction. That is like a doctor examining a patient without taking his or her pulse.

Why should an organization measure customer perceptions, expectations and satisfaction? Those factors are the heartbeat of your business.

Every client we have worked with in the past nine years said on the initial interview that customer satisfaction was an important part of their business strategy, yet few of those clients had in place a tool to accurately measure customer satisfaction. They do now.

One of the first things I do when I begin working with clients is help them develop and install an instrument for measuring customer satisfaction. Admittedly, it's easier, and perhaps more fun, to count dollars of income than it is to collect feedback and conduct quality and quantity analyses of customer satisfaction. Most organizations I work with, however, quickly come to depend on a customer satisfaction instrument as a management tool in implementing their Strategic Focus.

With a good measuring plan in place, your top-level management can look at the quantity of satisfaction — what percentage of your customers are happy with your service or with the product they bought from you; or, how many consumer complaints have you generated in the last year? And, they can look at the quality of your customer satisfaction — How loyal are your customers? What depth of satisfaction and enthusiasm do they feel for your product or service?

Assumptions Are Dangerous

Remember the old adage, "To assume means to make an ass out of you and me?" Many organizations which have concentrated on turnover, activity and income and have assumed that if those factors are favorable, customer satisfaction must certainly be all right have lived to respect the truth of the adage. A host of entrepreneurial competitors are always lurking out there looking for a crack in your competitive advantage. They'll manage to crawl into the smallest of openings and, like freezing action working on a giant boulder, expand and contract until they break you loose and you come crashing down like a rockslide in spring thaw.

Seven-Up with their assault on Coke and Pepsi is an example of a David going after Goliaths who were not alert. The cola giants did not fall, of course, but they sure had to scramble to meet the Seven-Up encroachment.

Remember that your best customers are always at the top of your competitors' "hot prospect" lists and that customer loyalty is relative.

You've probably heard people say, "Well, I'm a Chevrolet person, myself. I grew up in a Chevy. My dad and my granddad both drove Chevys, and I don't expect to ever own any other make."

Anyway, just let that fellow get hold of a lemon off the Chevy line or come upon a dealership that gives poor service, and see how loyal he is. He'll probably convert to the "Quality, is Job #1" company so fast it will make your head swim.

Your relationship with any customer is no better than that customer's latest encounter with your organization, and customer satisfaction is not a factor that the CEO can forget about as soon as he or she has assigned responsibility to a QA department or a customer service committee. Top management people need to be in direct contact with customers to handle complaints. They need to make sure they understand how customers feel toward the company.

For example, consider how effective this typical way of handling customer complaints is:

Many companies establish a rotating committee that includes one representative from each department in the organization. The various department heads are responsible for assigning personnel from their area to handle customer complaints.

The philosophy behind this type system is that all levels of employees will get a feel for the problems that can develop with consumers of the organization's product or service. That's an admirable philosophy. It's good for everyone to be aware of problems the company faces.

But consider what might happen if the person who is doing customer satisfaction surveys one week has to report information that reflects negatively on his or her department. That information may be altered by the time top management gets it.

How Can You Best Gauge Customer Satisfaction?

In our work with client organizations, we use the following four specific techniques that have proved effective in measuring customer satisfaction:

(1) Customer Satisfaction Survey

The Customer Satisfaction Survey is a paper and pencil instrument or a telephone survey used to get customer input on specific areas of their satisfaction.

We begin the process of developing such a tool by pulling together a project team from the client organization. The team members should be people who have experience with customers and have some understanding of what customers expect. If the company has done any market research, we would include someone familiar with the findings from that research.

Once we have the team in place, we use the storyboarding technique described in chapter seven to develop a list of customer-satisfaction elements unique to the organization. These are broad topics where customers have expressed some concern or expectation.

We then prioritize that list and identify the top twenty dimensions or elements of customer satisfaction. The next step is to develop a question relating to each of the dimensions through which the customer can evaluate the company on a scale of one to five.

Once the twenty questions are written, they are tested for validity, revised if necessary, and turned into a survey questionnaire. Demographic information such as age, sex, frequency of purchase and other such questions are frequently included in the survey, and space is provided for comments.

The project team usually considers at length the critical decision of survey implementation. Whether the questionnaires are distributed to customers in the place of business, sent through the mail, or handled by telephone may play a major role in both the number of responses you get and the accuracy of those responses.

A study of reported research on the question indicates that telephone surveys result in a higher level of response. I found, however, after digging into the use of telephone surveys, a lot of information that causes me to question the validity and advisability of depending on this type of research. The proliferation of telemarketing activity in recent years has caused many consumers to resist responding to these surveys. Many people have told me they give a telephone surveyor whatever information they think he or she wants to hear just to end the conversation quickly and courteously. Other people have criticized the quality of work done by telephone surveyors and say they question the reliability of data collected by these inexperienced callers.

My experience has been that, with careful planning, direct mail questionnaires can produce a very good response. When a well-written cover letter and a self-addressed stamped envelope are included, we have frequently gotten returns in the twenty-five percent to forry percent range. Statistically, this should give us valid information on which to base decisions.

We have also had some experience with distributing surveys in the client's place of business, such as at the check-out counter of a retail store. Of the three methods of collecting customer satisfaction information, I prefer mailing the survey to the customer and having him or her mail it back.

Once the survey questionnaire is returned, the data is compiled — usually entered into a computer — and the numeric information is tabulated. Numerical data by itself, however, gives an incomplete picture. A combination of the numerical data and the qualitative data — customer comments — is what helps us make valid decisions about customer satisfaction. The numerical data can be used to track customer satisfaction over time and to show whether the trend is favorable or unfavorable, but the comments give insight into the whys behind the figures.

(2) **Mystery Shopper Audit**

The mystery shopper audit also utilizes a survey format which can be effectively developed by storyboarding. The questionnaire for a shopping audit is much more detailed and asks for specifics such as the name of the sales person involved, the time and date of the transaction, specific observations of the behavior of key people involved in the sale, the appearance of the facility, timeliness of service and other issues.

A number of mystery shopper organizations around the country employ trained personnel to shop at and analyze the service of businesses. One such business, Shop'N'Chek, is headquartered in Atlanta, Georgia. Headed by Carol D. Cherry, Shop'N'Chek's focus is to capitalize on bad products and rude service. Her firm has more than 15,000 "shoppers" servicing several hundred accounts from department store chains to fast food houses.[1]

The Joseph B. Dahlkemper Company uses the mystery shopper audit as a basis for giving awards in their catalog showroom business. Each month, Dahlkemper's gives awards to individual sales counselors in the chain who achieve exceptional ratings in customer awareness. The company also uses the mystery shopper audit as a basis for coaching and training employees who consistently demonstrate a lack of customer awareness.

Like the customer satisfaction survey, data from the mystery shopper audit is both quantitative and qualitative. The quantitative data is tracked over time while the qualitative information is used to make specific modifications or corrections to the customer-service system.

(3) Letters to the President

A third tool through which to measure customer satisfaction is what's commonly called "letters to the president." A number of our clients use this technique to solicit specific comments about the level of customer service and satisfaction.

Typically, letters to the company head are qualitative in nature and require sorting through a variety of comments to draw valid conclusions.

Through my work with a variety of clients, I have developed a technique whereby we translate the twenty dimensions from an organization's customer-satisfaction survey for use in analyzing their letters to the president. We set up a computer program using the dimensions.

Someone on the customer-satisfaction project team is assigned to tabulate the results of each letter that comes in on the same one-to-five scale that is used on the survey form. The analyzer reads the letter thoroughly, isolating each individual comment and making a judgment about which of the twenty dimensions it should be ranked under. Positive comments receive a score of five. Negative comments score one. Each letter, of course, receives a response.

Again using Dahlkemper's as our example, we found that over a two-year period, the number of letters to the president consistently increased from quarter to quarter. The numerical index moved up slightly over the two-year period of our study but showed consistent dips in certain quarters of the year. Our analysis of the data indicated, for instance, that the company received fewer comments during the Christmas season and found it more difficult to measure customer satisfaction during that quarter.

Another interesting factor in the Dahlkemper's study was our measure of the ratio of positive to negative comments. We found, over the two-year period, that the index changed dramatically from two negative comments for every positive response to four positives for every one negative. We attribute the significant changes in those figures to two factors:

(A) Typically, people are more apt to write to company heads when they are dissatisfied with a product or service; but Dahlkemper's actively solicited letters, so they received both negative and positive ones.

(B) As a result of activity to measure customer satisfaction and to identify and isolate areas of concern and action to remedy deficiencies, the company affected a measurable improvement of service to its customers.

(4) **Focus Groups**

The use of focus groups is also a good technique for measuring customer satisfaction. A focus group is composed of ten to twelve customers who are willing to contribute an hour giving the organization feedback. An experienced group facilitator leads the discussion and helps document results.

Sessions can be documented through tape recordings or through storyboarding. I have found that the latter method is most effective. Storyboarding is an effective method of making visible the feedback from the various participants.

Focus groups allow for more thorough identification and development of weaknesses in customer satisfaction, because the setting allows for piggy-backing or hitch-hiking of ideas. If one member of the group brings up a topic of concern, other participants tend to expand on that point and help clarify the problem.

Inputs from focus groups can be quantified in the same manner letters to the president are. Comments from the focus group can be classified under your twenty categories, and a positive or negative judgment noted.

The real importance of utilizing a focus group, however, is in gathering concrete examples of customers' perceptions that allow you to take specific action.

Organizations that are focused on customer satisfaction usually use a combination, or all four, of these measuring techniques to gain a composite picture of their customers' satisfaction level. Our experience has shown that by combining all four tools and using both qualitative and quantitative evaluations, we are able to collect accurate information that will help an organization better serve its clients.

Sometimes Informal Measures Are Best

In addition to surveys and audits, letters, and focus groups, I have found numerous companies that also utilize informal satisfaction assurance systems to keep in touch with their customers.

H.O. Hirt, founder of the Erie Insurance Group in Erie, Pennsylvania, initiated a periodic letter on company stationery urging customers with problems to call the company collect. Hirt listed his office number on the letter and he personally accepted every phone call for many years. He even listed his home telephone number in the event a customer could not reach him during office hours.

As the company grew, it became more difficult for one person to answer all of the calls, but H.O.'s son William, current chairman of the board, still takes many customer calls.

Customer calls that come in to the Wachovia Bank and Trust CEO's office are handled right there under his supervision. They are not transferred "to the department that handles this type thing." If the problem cannot be solved immediately, the secretary contacts the customer with daily progress reports until the matter is settled.

J. W. Marriott, Sr., founder of the Marriott Corporation, was also noted for paying personal attention to customer satisfaction. He is reputed to have read every customer complaint or customer letter coming into the corporation and personally followed up to make sure corrective action was taken.

One company we know of has a system in place requiring each top company executive to contact five customers every Monday morning. The company representative does not call a purchasing agent in the customer company, but rather the line user of the company's machinery. He or she just asks, "How's it going?" "Are there problems with our equipment that we can help you solve?" This type of personal telephone contact goes a long way toward getting concrete, tangible information about customer service and product quality.

From the other side of the coin, top management people should be in direct contact with customers to handle complaints. Such contacts ensure that upper level executives understand how customers feel toward the company. Direct customer contact also provides an opportunity for executives to judge whether the organization's Strategic Focus is in focus.

When a large corporation with a lot of divisions really gets to perking and decision making is delegated throughout the organization, the Strategic Focus can easily get lost in the shuffle, so that corporate policies contradict the stated purpose.

Let's return to that shipping department example we used in an earlier chapter. If we suppose, for example, that the organization's Strategic Focus calls for creating a high quality image with the customer, we would expect the shipping agent to opt for a new, custom-designed box in which to ship a company product. However, if the department-level performance of the agent or supervisor is evaluated on the basis of how much money he or she saves the company, the cost of a new box poses a real conflict of interest at decision time.

Some corporate policies are set up for personnel evaluation and are based on one set of criteria, whereas, the Strategic Focus may be expressed in a totally different direction. When determining policy, you must continually ask, "Is the net effect of this policy consistent with the Strategic Focus?"

A story about service on a mass transit line exemplifies the problem. As the tale goes, busses on a particular run routinely failed to stop for passengers who were waiting at various designated pick-up points. In response to complaints about the practice, the route manager explained that if the busses had to stop at every pick-up, they would get off schedule.

KEY POINTS

(1) **Customer perceptions, expectations and satisfaction are the heartbeat of a business.**

(2) **With a good measuring tool in place,**

organizational management can assess both quantity and quality of customer satisfaction.

(3) Your best customers are always at the top of your competitors' "hot prospect" lists.

(4) Your relationship with any customer is no better than that customer's latest encounter with your organization.

(5) The four best ways to gauge consumer satisfaction are:

   (A) Customer Satisfaction Survey

   (B) Mystery Shopper Audit

   (C) Letters to the President

   (D) Focus Groups

(6) Top-level management must maintain direct customer contact.

(7) When determining company policy, keep the question uppermost in your mind: "Is the net effect of this policy consistent with the Strategic Focus?"

NOTES:
[1]"Small Business," *USA Today*, Sept. 11, 1987. Sec. B, p. 4.

Role of the Management Team in Guiding Strategic Focus

PURPOSE: *To give organizational management teams
specific ideas on how to guide
implementation of the Strategic Focus.*

In a "What's-in-it-for-me?" world, leadership has more to do with inspiration, communication and facilitation than it does with authority, control and decision-making.

Successful leadership is making the answers to the "What's-in-it-for-me?" question mutually beneficial for the customer, the employee and the owners of the corporation. This can happen only when management at all levels understands, is committed to, and has the skills to reconcile the conflicting needs and motivations that are constantly fighting against the Strategic Focus.

Top Management Guides the Execution of Strategic Focus

The role of top management in guiding the execution of the Strategic Focus includes bringing the guiding philosophy to life, helping develop skills and capabilities, insuring that systems are

171

in place to accomplish mission and goals and insisting on and rewarding excellence.

If you analyze organizations from IBM to McDonald's to Disney to the Dana Corporation, you will quickly see that those organizations have become successful because of the efforts of a charismatic leader who has developed, and brought to life, a strong guiding philosophy. The process, of course, involves a certain amount of drama. Leaders of successful organizations sometimes have to go out on a limb and ignore typical, acceptable management practices, but the result of a strong leader sticking his or her neck out often is that people come to understand and believe and buy into the guiding philosophy.

The Ren McPherson story is the classic example of charismatic leadership. During my tenure with the company, I heard the tale of the Dana policy sheet several times.

Earlier, in Chapter Three, I described how when McPherson assumed the company's leadership in the late 1960s, he found a very centralized, autocratic system in place. Espousing a different management philosophy himself, the new CEO decided he would have to either adjust to what he considered an ineffective system or take some dramatic steps to break the ingrained behavior patterns. He chose the latter.

McPherson called all the top executives into a room furnished with a U-shaped table, placed a large waste can in the middle of the floor, dumped the 22-inch-thick corporatepolicy manual into the can, set it afire and looked around at the shocked executives and asked how they would manage the company from that point forward.

The Executive Strategy Retreat which followed the burning of the company policies lasted many days and produced a new statement of philosophy for Dana Corporation. The document, known formally as "the policy sheet," was printed on one side of one sheet of paper — a far cry from the earlier voluminous document that had served as the company "discipline."

The Dana policy sheet is headed by the corporate goal of "Turning power into progress around the world" and is broken into the following major divisions:

(1) Earnings   (5) Organization
(2) Growth   (6) Customers
(3) People   (7) Communication
(4) Planning   (8) Citizenship

The sheet was revised eventually into "The 40 Statements," which is a series of short phrases describing specific corporate values in a fresh format. Rather than paragraphs under the eight headings listed above, the new document consisted of such statements as:

People are our most important asset.

People respond to recognition.

Freedom to contribute and opportunity to grow.

Wages and related benefits are the concern and responsibility of supervisors.

Keep no files.

Once McPherson had torched the company policies and guided the development of an understandable philosophy, he undertook the communicating of it. He spoke with corporate executives and operating managers at the home office and he visited about sixty outlying manufacturing and distribution facilities a year. He met with all the employees at each site, sharing and reinforcing their understanding of the company's purpose.

Evidently, McPherson recognized that simply writing a philosophy statement is not enough. You have to turn it into reality by demonstrating it, by living it and by repeating it; and when it becomes second nature to everyone in the organization, you will know that your people have become true believers.

The Barnes Group, based in Bristol, Connecticut, has done a good job of converting their people into believers.

Following an ESR in which Barnes' strategic-planning team developed a guiding philosophy statement focused on customer service, CEO Wally Barnes and company president Bill Fenoglio initiated a blitz. They introduced the new philosophy in group meetings that included every employee in the organization: All business units of the Barnes Group would focus on recognizable value-added service to the customer.

As a result of the top executives' interest, the mission caught on rapidly throughout the organization. The number of people who in fact understood the importance of the guiding philosophy accepted the basic premises of the idea and were willing to act on it was impressive. We followed the initial ESR and introduction of the purpose with strategy retreats in various operating units from Mississippi to Canada, and learned, without exception, that before we arrived on the scene, the subsidiary group had already bought into the big picture as a result of Barnes' and Fenoglio's earlier work. Members of the executive teams in the subsidiaries were familiar with the Barnes philosophy and had already begun to incorporate it into their day-to-day operations.

Ray Kroc, to whom we have referred so many times in this book, is famous for reinforcing the McDonald's organization's Quality, Service, Cleanliness and Value philosophy. He's notorious among his stores for driving up in a large limousine, picking up a paper cup from the parking lot and depositing it in the trash receptacle.

We see examples of what Tom Peters called "management by wandering around" in many successful organizations. What are the big cheeses doing when they wander around? They are making sure that the guiding philosophy comes to life throughout the organization.

Successful Top-Level Managers Guide Development of Skills and Capabilities

One of the critical ingredients of making any strategy work is the presence of the skills and capabilities within the organization to make it happen. That factor is not a given. It often has to be developed. Let's look first at people skills and capabilities then consider internal systems and procedures.

Alert CEOs realize they must not only have the skills and capabilities necessary to follow through on the focus, but must also communicate the importance of developing those facilities throughout the organization.

Long before they had adopted a strategic-planning philosophy, Joseph Dahlkemper and his wife, Lois, attended management-by-objectives seminars in their organization both to develop their own capabilities and to communicate to their employees the importance they placed on the training. In fact, when I was conducting management seminars at the company, Dahlkemper sat through the event twice, not because he was a slow learner, but because he wanted his people in each group to be aware of the value he attributed to the training.

It's important, I think, for managers at all levels to recognize that they're never finished learning and to support that attitude throughout their organization. To be effective, that leadership function must be approached from two directions: through presentations to and reinforcement of subordinates' learning throughout the company, and through continued development of the managers' skills and capabilities.

Dana's example of putting top executives on the resource staff of all training programs down through first-line supervisors in the manufacturing plants has paid dividends. Every training program the company conducted at Dana U included a lengthy visit from a top-level executive. Class participants were encouraged to engage the company exec in a shut-the-door, roll-up-your-sleeves discussion.

My own experience was that the sessions offered incredible learning opportunities. I was able to get insight into how executives of that caliber thought and was impressed with the importance the organization placed on training. Here was a $3 billion corporation (In the '70s) with more than 125 locations around the country, yet in any given week, at least two of the top fourteen executives could be found in a Dana University classroom talking to developing managers and supervisors about the organization.

According to Larry Lottier, Dean of the Business School at Dana University, "For many of the participants, this is their only opportunity to meet face to face with senior executives. It is one thing to hear about these people. It is something else to meet them, shake hands, ask questions, and have a drink together after class. It really makes an impression."

In many large corporations, the people out in the plants who make things happen never get to meet the executives at the top. At Dana, this opportunity is provided every time a manager or supervisor comes to a Dana U class. They go back to their plant feeling special. As Larry's little girl, Erin, said after returning from a trip to Walt Disney World, "Daddy, I met the real Mickey Mouse."

Dana also encouraged ongoing, informal learning cells called simply "discussion groups." Typically, the small groups met monthly with a senior executive who would describe how he or she had grown through the organization, relate some experiences and respond to questions and discussion.

As a reward for including these "big kids" in our elite group of high-potential young executives, we often allowed them to buy our dinner while we continued the discussion. It worked. Over a cocktail and dinner, we got to better understand the executive-development process, what was expected of organizational leaders, and that exec's perception of the organization and its mission. These sessions sometimes lasted until midnight.

Jim Wilcock, chief executive of Joy Manufacturing, also recognized the importance of and established a strong employee skills and capabilities development program. Art Mudge, vice president of value analysis for the company, put together a corporate-wide cost-improvement program that impressed Wilcock. When I left the company in 1978, sales were running about $200 million in the Mining Machinery Group. Cost-improvement suggestions in that group totaled 3.75% of sales, or nearly $8 million.

Wilcock really bought into the cost improvement strategy. To reinforce his support for the program, he attended recognition dinners twice a year at each location. Large numbers of people were trained every year in cost-improvement techniques. Mudge kept extremely detailed records of company activity in that area and was able to demonstrate graphically that as employee training increased in cost-improvement, so did company savings.

In a move to refocus energies at one point, the company removed funding for the cost-improvement training program only to see the savings fall off. When training in the field was resumed, so were the savings.

Joy's Mining Machinery president, Carl Heinz, demonstrated his support of human resource development by assisting in development of training programs for young executives, and even taught the classes at times.

There is no question that an important part of implementing organizational strategy includes developing employee skills and abilities to perform the company's service or to manufacture the product.

At Bowman Distribution, a Cleveland, Ohio, based unit of The Barnes Group, management education was a critical part of communicating the strategy. Working with Bart Ziurys, manager of International Market Development, we created a management development program called "Managing For Competitive Advantage." The program is designed to help middle managers understand the company's strategy, and to get them to buy in. It also helps them learn to think strategically.

The program has full top-executive support. Bill Fenoglio, president of The Barnes Group, addressed the opening session. He described the corporate approach to strategic thinking and reinforced the Guiding Philosophy. Then John Knapp, group vice president for Bowman Distribution, presented the Bowman Strategy.

Bowman is a leading supplier of components and supplies for the maintenance, repair and overhaul market. Their strategy focuses on selected target market segments and selling the benefits of "The Bowman System," a package of value-added services tailored to each market segment.

According to John Knapp, "We have never had a true strategic plan at Bowman U.S. before. I don't think what we have come up with is perfect yet. We have to work with it. It is going to evolve. The critical phase is to get our middle managers married into and committed to the plan. These are the folks who have to make it work."

"The planning approach we are going to employ is a circular approach. It represents an ongoing process that will build on itself."

"By getting middle managers involved early, Bowman Distribution has been able to get their input in finding ways to clearly identify selected target markets and to define the value-added services that will give the company a significant competitive advantage."

For Training to Be Effective, a Good System Must Be in Place

The third point of The Strategy Diamond™ is processes that enable people to serve the customer. In my experience implementing strategy and analyzing customer satisfaction, I have found repeatedly that breakdowns occur, not in an organization's philosophy or its people, but in its systems.

The banking industry provides a typical case of a system getting in the way of serving customers. The myth of the economy of scale has led many banks to centralize their data processing and back-office operations. The theory is if you combine the functions, you save money. The reality is that centralized data centers open opportunities for managers to establish their own policies and procedures "for efficiency's sake." And the result is difficulty for the customer. Branch customers with concerns or problems or who want some special information from these consolidated systems are usually advised that the branch cannot respond because "the system won't let us do that."

Companies concerned about customer service are more apt to take an approach opposite to consolidation. Under Jan Carlzon's direction, SAS, for instance, added systems to make the customer's life easier. Carlzon isolated the needs of business travelers as a viable focus for SAS and instigated systems to guarantee on-time departure and quick luggage pickup on arrival. The company bypassed the usual consolidation approach, trained their people to be alert to business travelers' needs and set up systems aimed at achieving their purpose.

At First Seneca Bank in Oil City, Pennsylvania, the strategy team recognized the need to provide superior customer service. As part of their "We Do Banking Right" program, First Seneca measured internal customer satisfaction to determine ways to make their systems more user and customer friendly. Departments evaluated the customer satisfaction level of other departments. Through this evaluation the bank was able to identify areas where the system breaks down or creates unnecessary work for front-line customer-contact people and to work internally at eliminating the hitches.

Watch an efficient organization in action sometime. Analyze the process. Let's look at McDonald's again. What happens when you approach one of the store's counters? The system is organized. Each step, from taking your order to cooking the burger and fries to dispensing your drink, is clearly thought out and flows smoothly. This is the only way to effectively operate a franchise. Kroc's organization created a prototype, developed a system for each step and debugged the system to make sure it was easily transferable from one location to another. They were then able to sell franchises that include the products, the people training and the systems to make them work effectively.

Effective Managers
Insist on and Reward Excellence

Former Secretary of State Dr. Henry Kissinger is known for his insistence on excellence in planning documentation. The story is told of an aide in Kissinger's organization who prepared a plan for the secretary. Kissinger reportedly asked the aide, "Is this the best plan that you can devise?" "Well," hesitated the assistant, "I'm sure, with a little more work, it would be better."

Kissinger returned the plan to him.

Two weeks later the aide resubmitted the plan for approval. After several days, the secretary called the aide into his office. "Is this really the best plan that you can recommend?" he asked.

Taken slightly aback, the aide mumbled that perhaps a point or two could be better defined, and left the office, plan under his arm, determined that he would develop a plan that anyone — even Henry Kissinger — would recognize as perfect.

The young man worked feverishly for several more weeks. Finally he finished the plan and proudly marched into his superior's office. He handed the plan to the secretary and braced himself for the inevitable.

"Is this really the very best plan that you can come up with?" Kissinger asked.

"Yes, Sir, Mr. Secretary," the aide answered assuredly.

"Good," Kissinger said. "In that case, I'll read it."

The key points from this story are:

(1) People can and will do better if they believe you expect them to.

(2) Mediocrity is not acceptable.

(3) CEOs must signal to the organization that only excellence and thoroughness are expected and accepted.

Not only is it important to expect and accept only excellence, but it is important to reward it.

Maybe you've heard the story of how the Foxboro Corporation's Gold Banana Award got started.

Foxboro is a maker of electronic instruments. Late one Friday afternoon, so the story goes, the Foxboro president was sitting in his office when a scientist from one of the research departments came down the hall with a new invention under his arm. The researcher had just made a major breakthrough and was looking for someone to share it with.

Because it was late Friday evening, the only person in the building was the president. The excited scientist was undaunted. He marched into the inner sanctum, plunked his invention down on the company president's highly polished desk and proceeded to explain the item with enthusiasm.

The president was so overcome by the fervor of this inventor that he wanted to give him an immediate reward. He searched through his desk to find something suitable to use for instant recognition. There were no company cuff links, no engraved pens in sight. The only thing he could find was a banana left from his lunch. He ceremoniously presented the inventor with the banana.

As you can imagine, the scientist's initial reaction was surprise. Later, as he described the incident to co-workers, the story was met first with laughter, then with insight. Foxboro employees who now receive "gold banana" pins cherish them as no other award.

Joe Dahlkemper is the only person in his company who can award an employee with the Gold Bee Award. The recognition is determined through letters to the president and mystery shopper audit reports. Once an employee has been designated to receive a Gold Bee, the founder plans a trip to that employee's showroom, gathers a number of other employees around and presents the award with much ceremony.

So, keep in mind that finding new and different ways to recognize excellence is important; and a little drama and show-manship goes a long way toward creating enthusiasm.

Middle Managers Play an Important Role in Executing Strategic Focus

Most middle management people are looking for reinforce-ment of their roles. They tend to be in that middle ground many people consider trivial.

A major trend exists throughout the business community to reduce middle management. It is called "leaning" or getting rid of the "tiering effect." A certain amount of cutting out the fat can be good, and in many organizations, it's long overdue. But once an organization passes twenty-five employees, a degree of middle management is crucial. The question is not whether, with twenty-five or more employees, you will have middle-level managers, but what your middle management should be doing.

Middle managers serve as a conduit for the free flow of ideas and information at all levels and in all directions throughout an organization. Consider the example of an old-fashioned water mill. Upper management is the resource pool necessary to oper-ate the wheel and grind the grain. Middle management is the sluice through which the water (energy, ideas, strategy) moves to operate the wheel. Front-line supervisors are analogous to the turning wheel which drives the grooved granite stones to pro-duce the flour. If it is channeled correctly, a small supply of water from the pond can cause big action in the gears and grind stones.

The middle manager's job includes elements from several

levels, such as planning, organizing, interpreting, directing, controlling, staffing and the formal application of skills involving equipment and functions as well as people. Middle managers have to be aware of the impact their style, their support or lack of it, even their mistakes have on the supervisory and worker levels of an organization. If the sluice springs a leak or gets knocked out of position, the wheel and the rest of the system don't function properly.

One of the ways to get middle managers involved is through education and training. Earlier, I mentioned our seminar called "Managing For Competitive Advantage." It is created especially for middle managers who report directly to members of the top executive strategy team.

The purpose of the seminar is to help managers understand the process of strategic thinking, to let them know what their bosses went through to develop the strategy, and to communicate the strategy. We also want to help managers prepare a plan for their own areas of responsibility that is linked to the corporate strategy. One interesting exercise is to identify the "Barriers to Strategic Success." These are obstacles that get in the way of implementation, as seen from the middle managers' perspective.

To date, several hundred managers from a dozen different organizations have been through this exercise. The results show that the top six barriers are (1) lack of focus, (2) inadequate definition of strategy, (3) lack of coordination between departments, (4) lack of clear and complete vertical communication, (5) failure to realize that actions speak louder than words, and (6) lack of commitment.

Middle managers are charged with translating an organization's vision and mission into "bite-sized" tasks and action steps and facilitating their execution. They work at a fast pace and must handle decisions on widely diverse issues at an instant's notice. They act as customer advocates in all changes, disputes and conflicts.

Middle managers establish standards and monitor all systems, changes and actions for adherence to the Strategic Focus. They must make decisions on policy exceptions as they arise while they are also handling such routine duties as recognitions, ribbon cuttings and retirement parties. Middle-level managers are the company people who take the telephone calls, attend meetings, make presentations, greet visitors and go home late.

And now, many so-called management experts are saying that American corporations are cumbersome and ineffective and experience high overhead costs due to an overload in middle-level management. The idea is to cut the overhead by getting rid of middle managers.

The traditional role of middle managers seems to have been reading other people's reports and compiling new reports — reports that often nobody pays any attention to. True, that is a totally useless function. But if middle managers are properly directed, they can be of tremendous help to an organization.

Bill Gates, creator of the fast-growing computer programs company, Microsoft, believes in middle management. He recognized that the day-to-day running of the business kept him so bogged down in minutiae that he could not concentrate on the company's Strategic Focus, which was creating and marketing new software products for the computer industry. Various levels of managers, as Gates discovered, can take the pressure off a CEO so he or she can focus on developing new products and new marketing strategies. This function is especially crucial in an industry where new products or services are vital to the Strategic Focus.[1]

Front-Line Supervisors Know Where the Action Is

Many people consider front-line supervisors the most crucial element of the management cycle because they are the last link in the chain between top management and line workers. If the system breaks down at the front line, no amount of strategizing, or anything else, will make a difference.

Front-line supervisors are charged with translating the organization's Strategic Focus into specific language that employees can understand and get excited about. If a supervisor, for example, translates the latest communique on the organization's Strategic Focus as "another one of the old man's hair-brained ideas," you can forget any enthusiasm among the line workers who work under him or her.

On the other hand, if that supervisor really captures the spirit of the focus and has the ability to translate it into meaningful terms for the line workers, it can be a powerful force for the company.

Consider what could happen on the maternity wing of a large hospital if the housekeeping staff did not catch the spirit. After all, what's the point of cleaning up around a bunch of squalling, spitting babies? With recent changes in maternity care and relaxed visitation practices, daddies and granddaddies and toddling brothers and sisters roam all over the place, dropping cracker crumbs and chicken pox germs indiscriminately as they go. And, since in three days the baby will go home to that kind of environment anyway, why worry?

Under such circumstances, hospital housekeepers might be tempted to slosh along from room to room with a pail of dingy mop water, take a few swipes here and there, and move on. It's the front-line supervisor who can make a difference.

Supervisors who really buy an organization's purpose concentrate on creating a sense of urgency about customer focus and problem-solving activities, they initiate systems that free workers to perform at peak capacity, and in their spare time, they monitor product quality, customer service and individual performance.

Remember also that supervisors are the first link in the communication chain by which ideas and complaints of line workers flow upward. It will be the line supervisor, who will, for example be the first to detect whether most employees either don't understand or are not buying the Strategic Focus. And the line supervisor is in the best position to find out why the breakdown occurs.

It's not surprising then that the line supervisor's job is considered one of the most frustrating of all management functions. Supervisors hear directly the dissatisfaction of all levels of management above and the dissatisfaction of all the line workers below.

I recently heard about a line supervisor who had had a rough day and decided to check the situation on the home front before leaving the office. After all, he was considered line supervisor at home too, and sometimes dissatisfaction reached a pretty high level in the family room by nightfall. He called his wife and said, "I will come home if you promise not to fuss at me about anything. I feel like everybody I have talked to today was upset about something I could do nothing about."

KEY POINTS

(1) **Leadership has more to do with inspiration, communication and facilitation than it does with authority, control and decision-making.**

(2) **Leadership occurs only when management at all levels understands, is committed to and has the skills to reconcile conflicting needs and motivations.**

(3) **The role of top management in guiding the execution of the Strategic Focus includes bringing the philosophy to life, helping develop skills and capabilities, insuring that systems are in place to accomplish goals and insisting on and rewarding excellence.**

(4) **Managers at all levels must recognize that they're never finished learning, and they must support that attitude throughout their organization.**

(5) **Most breakdowns occur, not in an organization's philosophy or its people, but in its systems.**

(6) **Not only is it important to expect and accept only excellence, but it is important to reward it.**

(7) **Middle managers serve as a conduit for the free flow of ideas and information at all levels and in all directions throughout an organization.**

(8) **Front-line supervisors are charged with translating the organization's Strategic Focus into specific language that employees can understand and get excited about.**

NOTES:

[1]Anne R. Field, "Managing Creative People," *Success*, (Oct. 1988), 85-87.

AFTERWORD

It Takes Work

Now that we have been through all of this, I realize I probably have not told you a lot that you did not already know. Perhaps, however, I have given you some specifics and ideas which you can use to focus your own thinking.

The crucial question at this point is "What are you going to do with the information I have shared with you?" If there's one indisputable fact about Strategic Focus, it is that focusing doesn't happen automatically. You have to make it happen.

Good luck, and I hope you and your stakeholders catch the spirit of your mission and that your Strategic Focus becomes so sharp that you overtake and bypass all of your competitors on your journey to the marketplace. After all, that is what developing and acting on a clear Strategic Focus is all about.